JEWS OF LITHUANIA AND LATVIA: THE GRAUDANS

DISCOVERY TO DIASPORA

AuthorHouse™
1663 Liberty Drive
Bloomington, IN 47403
www.authorhouse.com
Phone: 1-800-839-8640

First published by AuthorHouse   7/15/2011

ISBN: 978-1-4634-2076-5 (sc)
ISBN: 978-1-4634-2075-8 (e)

Library of Congress Control Number: 2011911544

Printed in the United States of America

Any people depicted in stock imagery provided by Thinkstock are models,
and such images are being used for illustrative purposes only.
Certain stock imagery © Thinkstock.

This book is printed on acid-free paper.

Because of the dynamic nature of the Internet, any web addresses or links contained in this book may have changed
since publication and may no longer be valid. The views expressed in this work are solely those of the author and do
not necessarily reflect the views of the publisher, and the publisher hereby disclaims any responsibility for them.

JEWS OF LITHUANIA AND LATVIA: THE GRAUDANS

DISCOVERY TO DIASPORA

KEITH W. KAYE

authorHOUSE®

Other Books by Keith W. Kaye

Illustrated Diary of a Romantic Prussian Soldier (with Thomas R. Heysek)

Man of Tempered Steel – Bruno Schlesinger (Helga Kaye with Keith W. Kaye)

Johanna Holzberg c.1856-1928 (South Africa)

Dr. Moritz Graudan 1856-1922 (Europe)

Rocha Friedlander 1861-1941 (Europe)

Sarah Quasser 1878-1950 (America)

The Founding Graudan Siblings

Dedication

As always, to my Parents, the late Professor Josse Kaye and Helga Kaye (b. Schlesinger), for their love, guidance, support and enduring example.

To my Wife, Dr Valda Kaye, for her love, friendship, companionship and incredible generosity of spirit.

To our Children, Jessica, Deborah, and Maxine for their love and friendship, and for turning out to be such beautiful young women, in both body and soul; adventurous, exciting, passionate, dedicated and hard working.

And finally to all the Graudan Family and all those interested in their family history; and for all those to come.

This is for you.

Contents

Acknowledgments

First and foremost, I'd like to thank my wife Valda and our children Jessica, Deborah, and Maxine for their support and encouragement. To my sister Rea Gardy and niece Tanya for all of their help with editing and proofreading, and for their wise suggestions. To my cousin Jean Michel Linois for his passion in exploring his origins. Without him, this work would not exist and the Graudan Family would have faded away, like dissolving shadows, into oblivion.

My special thanks to . . . Leonardo Herzenberg for his tremendous skill in translating the memoirs of his father Robert Herzenberg, and for so kindly permitting me to reproduce these; also to the amazing gracious and generous manner in which Dr. Edward Anders permitted me to use his work and for obtaining permission from the family of the late Solomon Feigerson; to my cousin Ruthie Kalin for so kindly entrusting me with her most precious old photographs and the diary from her grandmother Sarah Quasser. All of you have enabled the world to clearly see and remember some of the good times the Lithuanian and Latvian Jews, and especially the Graudan Family, must have experienced, and also the difficulties and tragedies they had to endure. Through your work their times and names will never be forgotten.

All the Graudan Family for providing information, stories, and photographs, and for suffering my repeated emails and phone calls. Thank you, Jeanne and Dr. Scott Hollington, for creating such beautiful maps and contributions for the cover. Thank you, Susan Kay Wilson, for your meticulous typing.

Author Note: I have used the old German/Yiddish names of Libau and Ponevas almost interchangeably with the modern Latvian/Lithuanian/English terms Liepāja and Panevezys as these were the way most of us heard and read about the cities from our families.

List of Illustrations

Chapter 8

Appendix 2

Appendix 3

Introduction

Paris, summer 2008.

My wife Valda and I had flown to Paris for a long weekend from Minneapolis, Minnesota, USA. Our youngest daughter, Maxine, was studying French. While wandering the streets of this beautiful city, Maxine asked: "Dad, do we have any relatives in France?"

"Sorry Max, none at all."

For the next three days we did what tourists do in Paris—we had fun, visited museums, shopped at local stores, ate out at restaurants, and enjoyed one memorable picnic alongside the Seine.

Arriving home from the airport in Minneapolis, I went straight to the mailbox. There was a handwritten envelope with a French stamp, addressed: "Personal Attention of Mr. Keith Woodhill Kaye." Intrigued, I tore it open.

> Dear Mr. Kaye,
>
> Please accept my apologies in case the following lines do not appear to have been directed to the intended person. Along with my American cousins, we have been trying to locate our South African cousins for quite some time. All of us trace our family roots back to Latvia, to the city of Libau (currently Liepāja). After tedious research in our family records and investigations in the South African Archives, I was able to "reconstruct" what seems to be the South African limb of the family tree and you happen to be the first person I could find that seems very likely to be our contemporary cousin.

The writer then went on to describe, in great detail, many aspects of my Graudan family that were known to me, but he also brought to my attention many new aspects. He then concluded:

> . . . With this (too) long explanation, I sincerely hope you will be able to determine whether our families are indeed closely related—we are looking forward, if this is the case, to a warm welcome in our midst. There are exciting possibilities!
>
> Yours sincerely,
> Jean Michel Linois

My response by email was:

> Tuesday, June 24, 2008, 10:30:26AM.
>
> Dear Jean Michel,
> I am truly delighted to hear from you! The world works in weird and wonderful ways! I received your most charming letter yesterday, just as I returned to Minneapolis from . . . Paris. My wife and I went to Paris for a rushed, but wonderful, three-day trip to visit our daughter Maxine, who is studying French. Had I received your letter before we left I would have stayed on so we could meet.
>
> I have asked Maxine to contact you. She has been in France for six weeks and is due to remain in Paris for another two weeks, before traveling a bit and then returning to University in New York in late July. I sincerely hope she can meet you, Anne, Emmanuel, and Raphael. Max is twenty-five and, sorry if I sound like a boasting father, but she is a delightful, fun young woman. One request, please: Please try to talk to her only in French. She is trying to be fluent, but her friends are talking to her more in English.

B.logne (France), 15-06-08

Personal attention of
M. Keith Woodhill KAYE
263 Peninsula Road
Minneapolis - MN-55441
(USA)

Dear M. KAYE,

please accept my apologies in case the following lines do not appear to have been directed to the intended person.

Along with my American cousins, we have been trying to locate our South African cousins for quite some time. All our us trace our family roots back in Latvia, in the city of LIBAV (currently LIEPAJA).

After tedious research in our family record and investigations in the South African Archives, I was able to "reconstruct" what seems to be the South African limb of our family tree and you happen to be the first person I could find that seems very likely to be our contemporary cousin.

If I guessed right, our common ancestor is Israel GRAUDAN, probably born around 1830 in LIBAV. He had 2 sons and 3 daughters: Dr. Moritz GRAUDAN (deceased in 1922), Nicolas GRAUDAN (who died at age 15), Sarah GRAUDAN (1878 - 1952) who married M. Isaac QUASER, Rocha (Rachel) GRAUDAN (1861 - 1941) who married M. Samuel FRIEDLAENDER, and finally, Joanna GRAUDAN who married M. Julius HOLZBERG.

— Rocha GRAUDAN - FRIEDLAENDER was my great-grandmother. She fell victim of the Shoah in Latvia in 1941.

— Joanna GRAUDAN - HOLZBERG emigrated to South Africa in the late 1890s. She is believed to have given birth to 2 Boys and 2 girls: Adolf Theodore, Tom, Minnie (1879 - 1957) and Rebecca (1879 - 1933). We have pictures of Adolf Theodore and Tom (Tommie) in our family archives that taken while they were already living in South Africa.

TSVP→

XVI.

Jean Michel, I must congratulate you on your most amazing research. I really look forward to hearing all about you, your family, and how you managed to get all the information! I, too, am most interested in the family history and have details of the South African descendants of our common great-great-grandparents Israel and Hinda Etta Graudan. . . . Looking forward to hearing from you further, especially if Maxine can get to meet you soon.

With warmest regards,
Keith

I also emailed Max; but I sent the message to the wrong address!

From Jean Michel:

Tuesday, June 24, 2008.

Dear Keith,
Too bad we missed you in Paris! I'm just baffled that we managed to establish this amazing connection in the first place. That your answer was posted on my email box the very evening I'm returning from Israel. That so many years of oblivion and disconnection due to the Shoah were erased by a miracle. G-d's ways are, indeed, mysterious; let me first tell you that when I read your letter to my wife Anne and our 2 sons Emmanuel (eighteen) and Raphael (fourteen) half an hour ago, we jumped out of joy. Be assured that your daughter Maxine is most welcome. She needs to know that she will be considered as a member of our family at home. Our new additions to our scattered "mishpokhe" is so precious, indeed. We will commit to speaking to her in French, as you recommended, so she can improve her command of the language. It's midnight, so I will stop for now and will get back to you tomorrow after a good sleep.

Take care, Kindest Regards,
Jean Michel & Anne + the boys

Wednesday, June 25, 2008.

Dear Keith,
I just called your daughter Maxine. She was flabbergasted by the news; she had not heard back from you but she was apparently delighted to get to know her French cousins while in Paris! She will come home for dinner tomorrow. We look forward to it, as you can imagine.

Kindest Regards,
Jean Michel

Next, in True, Delightful Max form, I received a brief email:

Dad! Some guy claiming to be your cousin just called.
He lives in a nice part of Paris; so I am going to visit him!

Love you,
Max

When Max visited the Linois' she received a wonderfully warm welcome and apparently one of her comments to Jean Michel was, "My dad is also going to be thrilled this family discovery has been made. The only thing is, he is going to be somewhat pissed that you found him, before he found you!"

It was strange that, of all people, Jean Michel had picked me as the first family member to approach. I have been the one most interested in the family history and genealogy. Such chance, synchronicity, coincidence, luck, or, as some would have it, The Hand of G-d or Hashem; and this was not the end of it. From this happenstance seed—fertilized by modern technology of the Internet—phone and air travel has since developed a coming together of the three main branches of the Graudan Family from South Africa, Europe, and the United States.

This is their story.

CHAPTER 1

Discovering Panevezys:
Lithuanian Origin of Latvian Family

The summer prior to Jean Michel ferreting out the South African family branch, I had been on a family exploration of my own to discover my Baltic roots. Growing up, all I knew from my father, Josse (born Josiah Kaplan), was that his father, my grandfather (also Josiah Kaplan) had been born in "Russia." It is not traditional among Ashkenazy Jews for the father and son to have the same name. This always had to be explained by the fact that my grandfather had died when my father was five days old, before he was named.

The key to opening the mystery of the Kaplan side of my family came from a somewhat inauspicious dinner meeting at a restaurant in Johannesburg a few months earlier. A cousin, Winston Miller, and his sister Penny Davis (at that stage I had no idea how we were related) produced an old newspaper cutting from a 1934 Baltimore newspaper under the heading, "Catching Up With The Past 35 Years" (Fig. 1.1). Jenny Schutz (born Kaplan) was their grandmother, but we did not know if she was related to my grandfather Josiah—and if so, how. This was, however, the first inkling that maybe "Russia" was not the Russia we know today. What was initially a most enjoyable evening was marred, in that afterwards Penny could not find her handbag. A furtive couple sitting alongside us had managed to remove it from Penny's chair while she was looking at a slide presentation I had prepared. I felt really guilty and partly to blame. The couple was seen later, on closed-circuit television, leaving the building with something tucked under their clothing. Later the remnants of the bag were found strewn on a highway.

After this seemingly unpropitious meeting, extensive research both in South Africa and Lithuania confirmed one of my suspicions. The "Russia" my father had spoken about turned out to be The Russian Federation of the nineteenth century. And the place of origin of the Kaplans was Panevezys, the fifth largest city in Lithuania.

The story of Josse's mother, Rebecca, was slightly better known. He had often told me that, "She was from Libau, which was in Kurland (wherever that might be) and the Jews of Kurland always thought of themselves as somewhat better than Jews from the surrounding areas." That was it! That was all we knew about the origins of my fathers' side of the family. Even these sketchy details were confused somewhat when I spoke to my father's last surviving sibling, his half brother Edwin Lichtenstein. Edwin had been ten years old when his mother died. He thought she was from a place called Orel, in Russia. Researching this turned out to be a dead end.

Eventually it was fairly easy to confirm, from the Latvian State Archives, that Rebecca had been born in Libau and that this was the old name for the modern Latvian city of Liepāja. Also, Liepāja is, indeed, in an area known as Kurland.

Around this time, in early 2007, I was put in contact with Howard and Esther Margol, a remarkable couple from Atlanta. About fourteen years ago they had started an organization called "The Foundation for Lithuanian and Latvian Jews." Besides its avowed purpose of helping modern Jews living in these Baltic States, they had also been running an annual trip to visit these historic sites. This was exactly what I needed. Indeed, Howard provided me with all the information and contacts for the Archives of Lithuania and Latvia so that by the time we got there, in summer 2007, I could be as prepared as possible. Delving into the Kaplan Lithuanian side of the family, I managed to make significant progress from the Internet, and was informed by the Lithuanian Archives that when we visited them they would have much more information as well as several documents for me.

The Latvian Archives informed me that they, too, had some information regarding the Graudan/Holzberg families. I sent the required funding and then heard nothing further until the day we were to leave the USA. I was informed the documents were ready to be collected from the Archives in Riga. The only problem was I was not going to Riga! The only part of Latvia I was going to was Liepāja. Eventually, after several desperate emails and calls, they agreed to send the documents to me in Liepāja.

Figure. 1.1 Baltimore Evening Sun 1934

The drive, with my Russian–Jewish interpreter and guide Daniel Gurevich, from Panevezys, Lithuania, to Liepāja, Latvia, took about three hours. I enjoyed the scenery, which was somewhat flat like Minnesota and talked to Daniel, mainly about growing up in the Soviet Union as a Jew with no religion. Going through my mind this whole time wasthe concept that these must have been very similar sights to those my family must have seen so many years ago. Maybe they even saw the exact same hillocks or copse of trees. I also was excited to imagine what the awaiting package would reveal. I was not disappointed.

Upon opening the envelope from the Latvian State Archives, two photographs spilled out, followed by a summary of the archival findings (Fig. 1.2). The summary detailed a series of individuals whom, at this stage, I could not readily place on the family tree. The photographs were from the Passport Issuance Books of Liepāja Prefecture for 1927 and 1928. One was of Rocha Friedlender (born Graudan on June 19, 1861, in Panevezys, Lithuania) and the other was her daughter Jenny (born January 1, 1900, in Libau). Rocha looked eerily similar to the photographs I had seen of my great-grandmother Johanna Holzberg (born Graudan). I surmised they were sisters. Of great interest was the fact that Rocha had been born in Panevezys. Could this somehow be the connection between my grandmother Rebecca from Libau and grandfather Josiah from Panevezys?

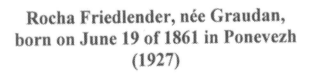

Rocha Friedlender, née Graudan, born on June 19 of 1861 in Ponevezh (1927)

Jenny Friedlender, born on January 1 of 1900 in Libau (1928)

Figure. 1.2 Passport photos of Rocha and daughter Jenny

Of even greater immediate interest was the statement from the archives, "Before the Second World War, Rocha along with her daughter Jenny Friedlender lived in Liepāja at Uliha Street 11, apartment 6 and in 1941 at apartment 3, 38 Toma Street" (Figs. 1.3, 1.4). My heart pounded. Could these buildings still be in existence? Could I witness the buildings in which these hazy, barely discernable, possible relatives had lived? So began my exploration of Libau, an almost hallowed name in my mind. Little did I know where this would lead. Would my journey bring great moments of understanding, joy, interest, happiness, and family gatherings? Or would it bring despair, sorrow, grief, and controversy?

LATVIJAS VALSTS ARHĪVU ĢENERĀLDIREKCIJA

LATVIJAS VALSTS VĒSTURES ARHĪVS

Reģ. Nr. 000302475, Slokas iela 16, Rīga, LV-1007. Tālr. 7613118

29. 05.2007   3-K-1855 N
_____ Nr. _____

Keith W Kaye MD

Uz _____

263 Peninsula Road
Medicine Lake
MN 55441
USA

ARCHIVAL REFERENCE
about Holzberg family

The birth, marriage and death records of the Jewish community in Libau (now Liepaja) for 1854-1905, the lists of the Jewish families, originated not from Courland, but living in Libau, set up in 1889, in 1893 and in 1896 contain the following information:

Joel (Jewel, Jowel) Herz, son of Itzik Holzberg from Salanty was born in ca 1854/1855 (aged 23 in 1878, aged 35 in 1889).
His wife **Hana Dische (Anna, Hanna), née Graudan** was born in ca 1856/1857 (aged 21 in 1878, aged 33 in 1889).
Their marriage was registered on March 28 of 1878 in Libau (see Appendix No.1).

They had children:
- daughter **Mina Holzberg**, born on January 2 of 1879 in Libau (see Appendix No.2).
- daughter **Betty Holzberg**, born in ca 1880 in Libau (aged 9 in 1889) (unfortunately the birth records of the Jewish community in Libau for 1879-1880 do not contain information on her birth) (we suppose Betty and Rebecca was one and the same person),
- son **Abram Abe (Abel) Holzberg**, born on March 31 of 1882 in Libau (see Appendix No.3),
- son **Isay-Kalman Holzberg**, born on October 26 of 1884 in Libau (see Appendix No.4).

According to the Inhabitants lists for 1889 Joel (Jewel) Holzberg lived in Libau since March 1881, his occupation – shop assistant (see Appendix No.5).
In the lists, set up in 1893, 1896 the family of Joel Holzberg was not registered.

Israil (Israel, Asriel), son of Owsey Graudan (other spelling Grauden, Graudon) from Ponevezh (now Lithuania), born in ca 1834. Occupation – corn trader.
His wife **Hinda-Eta, daughter of Abel** (maiden name is not stated) was born in ca 1835 (aged 59 in 1894).

In 1886 they lived in Libau at Schiffer (Kugu) Street in the house of Sachs. The family of Israil Graudan lived in Libau at least since 1878.
Israil Graudan died on February 7 of 1893 in Libau, aged 59.

Figure 1.3. Summary of Latvian Archival Findings May 2007. Page 1

Hinda-Eta Graudan died on August 13 of 1894 in Libau, aged 59 (see Appendix No.6-7).

Besides daughter Hanna they had at least two daughters:

- **Rocha Graudan**, born in ca 1870 (aged 25 in ca 1895). On May 14 of 1895 in Libau she married to a widower **Samuel, son of Abram Friedlender** from Pilten, born in ca 1855 (aged 39 ¾ in 1895). According to the Passport Issuance Books of Liepaja Prefecture for 1927 Rocha Friedlender, née Graudan was born on June 19 of 1861 in Ponevezh (we would like to draw your attention to the fact that very often the age of persons was determined by their outward appearance and was stated in some documents rather approximately) . Samuel Friedlender was born in 1854 in Pilten. Samuel died on June 1 of 1938 in Liepaja. Before the Second World War Rocha with daughter **Jenny Friedlender**, born on January 1 of 1900 in Libau, lived in Liepaja at Uliha Street 11, apt. 6. In 1941 at Toma Street 38, apt. 3 (see photos of Rocha and Jenny from the Passport Issuance Books of Liepaja Prefecture for 1927, 1928).

- **Sara (Sore) Graudan,** born in ca 1871 (aged 23 in 1894). On June 5 of 1894 in Libau she married to **Itzik, son of Josel Kwaser** from Shkudi (now Lithuania), born in ca 1867 (aged 27 in 1894).

REFERENCE: fond 5024, inventory 1, files 97, 99, 106, inventory 2, file 502,
fond 491, inventory 1, file 15, page 104,
fond 4350, inventory 2, files 1, 3,
fond 96, inventory 6, files 1163, 1201,
fond 412, inventory 7, file 421,
fond 5050, inventory 2, files 4548, 4746.

Enclosure: copies of the documents – 12 sheets.

Director   N. Rižovs

Head of Department   I. Veinberga

Figure 1.4. Summary of Latvian Archival Findings May 2007. Page 2

Earliest Known Groidam/Graudans
(5th to 3rd Great-Grandparents)

The earliest known members of the family were all found in the Lithuanian Archives, not the Latvian Archives, and the names were initially spelled as Groidam (Fig. 2.1).

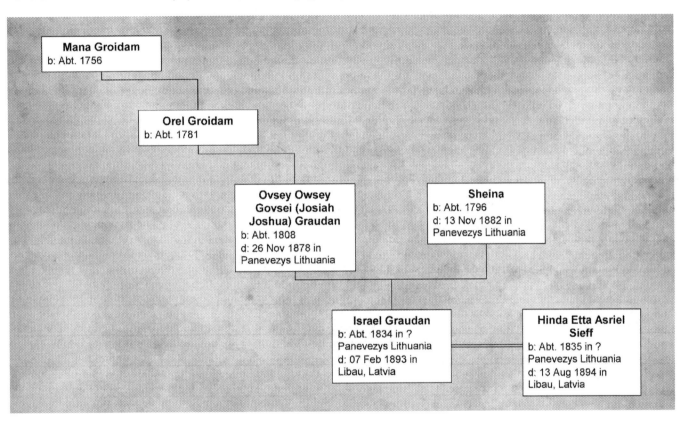

Figure 2.1. Earliest Groidam / Graudans from Lithuania

Mana Groidam (born abt 1756)

Authors' fifth great-grandfather (great-great-great-great-great-grandfather).

The earliest Graudan on record is Mana Groidam, in which he is stated as being the father of Orel Groidam. This was found in the Main Revision List of the Panevezys Jewish Community of April 20, 1834. The entry is written as, "Groidam Orel ben Mana fifty-three years old." If we assume Mana was twenty-five years old when his son Orel was born Mana would have been born around 1756. There was no evidence as to his wife's name (Fig. 2.2).

Figure 2.2. Letter from Lithuanian State Archives. Mana and his son Orel Groidam

Orel Groidam (born abt 1781) first wife unknown; second wife Khane

Authors' fourth great-grandfather (great-great-great-great-grandfather).

There are two records mentioning Mana's son Orel.

1. **Main Revision List of the Panevezys Jewish Community (April 20, 1834).**

During this time, Orel was fifty-three years old. "Groidam Orel ben Mana, fifty-three years old, and his [second?] wife Khane, thirty-two years old. His daughters Khaia, sixteen years old, and Eige, thirteen years old, and son Vigder, nine years old."

Orel would have been born around 1781. At this stage, in 1834, he was married to Khane, age thirty-two (b. abt 1802), who was probably his second wife. He had two daughters (presumably by his first wife): Khaia, age sixteen (therefore b. abt 1818), and Eige, age thirteen (therefore b. abt 1821). He also had one son, Vigder age nine (b. abt 1825), by either his first wife or by Khane (Fig. 2.2).

2. **His Son Ovsey's Death Record** (Panevezys Cemetery Records of 1872–1940). His son Ovsey died in Panevezys, at the age of seventy in 1878 (Fig. 2.4).

We can assume Orel was born around 1780 if he was about twenty-eight when his son Ovsey was born close to 1808. We also imagine he must have been living in Panevezys, as this was where his son lived and died.

Ovsey, Owsey, Govsei (Josiah, Joshua) Graudan (born abt 1808) and wife Sheine

Author's third great-grandparents; (great-great-great-grandparents).

Our next generation is Ovsey Graudan and his wife Sheine. He was the son of Orel and was born around 1808, probably in Panevezys. He definitely died in Panevezys. There are records that he died of Typhus Fever on November

26, 1878, and is buried in the Panevezys Jewish Cemetery. His whole life was spent within the Russian Empire.

There are four records for Ovsey.

1. **Main Revision List of the Panevezys Jewish Community (April 20, 1834).**

"Govsei twenty-three years with wife Sheine twenty-nine years old and Daughter Khave seven years old."

From this list, Graudan Family is written as "Groidam." Also according to the 1834 record, Govsei was twenty-three years old at the time. His date of birth therefore would be 1811. According to the cemetery records, it was 1808 (Fig. 2.3).

LIETUVOS VALSTYBĖS ISTORIJOS ARCHYVAS
LITHUANIAN STATE HISTORICAL ARCHIVES
Gerosios Vilties g. 10, 03134 Vilnius, Lithuania tel. ,
fax , e-mail: g.baranova@lvia.lt
Keith W. Kaye 2009-07-03

I have found the Graudan families written as Groidam and registered in the main <u>Revision List of April 20, 1834 of Panevezys Jewish Community</u>:

Govsei 23 years old with wife Sheine 29 years old and Daughter Khave 7 years old.

Galina Baranova (LIETUVOS VALSTYBĖS ISTORIJOS ARCHYVAS)

Figure 2.3. Letter from Lithuanian State Archives. Owsey and his wife Sheine Graudan

2. **His Death Record** (Panevezys Death Records 1872–1880).

The documented death of Panevezys town-dweller Ovsei ben Orel Graudan was caused by Typhus Fever on the November 26, 1878, when he was seventy years old. Ovsey is buried in what was the Panevezys Jewish Cemetery. This cemetery record is the first spelling of the name as "Grauden." From the revised cemetery list (1834) record he was "Govsei Groidam" (Fig. 2.4).

Surname	First	Father	Age	Date Death	Cause Death	Spouse	LVIA #
Grauden	Ovsey	Orel	70	26.11.1878	Typhus Fever	Sheina	1226/1/1127
Grauden	Sheina		86	13.11.1882	Lung Catarrah	Ovsei	1226/1/1310

This cemetery record is the first spelling as Grauden. From the Revison List 1834 record he was Govsei Groidam

Figure 2.4. From the Panevezys Death Records 1872–1880

3. **Latvian State Archives: List of Jewish Families Originated Not from Courland but Living in Libau** (set up in 1889, 1893, and 1896).

"Israil (Israel, Asriel) son of Owsey Graudan from Ponevezh" (Fig. 4.2).

4. **Family List 1908 of Panevezys Jewish Community**, as being the father of Izrel and Manel.

"Graudan Izrel ben Ovsei" and "Graudan Manel ben Ovsei." It is unclear why details of Izrel and his family are still in the Panevezys List of 1908 when by this stage the Graudan family had left Lithuania and had spread far and wide.

Sheine (born abt 1796 or 1805)

Two Records.

1. Main Revision List of Panevezys Jewish Community (April 20, 1834).

"Govsei twenty-three years old with wife Sheine twenty-nine years old and Daughter Khave seven years old." If Sheine was twenty-nine years old in 1834, she would have been born in 1805 (Fig. 2.3).

2. Panevezys Cemetery Records (1872–1940).

Sheina died November 13, 1882, at age eighty-six. Therefore, she would have been born abt 1796 (Fig. 2.4).

There is a nine-year age discrepancy between the 1834 list and the 1882 Panevezys Cemetery Records. Interestingly, however, in both records Sheine is older than her husband. Per the cemetery records: Sheina (b. abt 1796) and Ovsey (abt 1808)—twelve years older; and in the revised list: Sheine (born abt 1805) and Ovsey (abt 1811)—six years older.

Israel, Izrel, Israil, Asriel Graudan (born abt 1834) and wife Hinda Etta Sieff (born abt 1835)

The author's great-great-grandparents

CHAPTER 3

Lithuanian Jews and the Graudan Family in Panevezys

Lithuania has both the brightest stars and darkest clouds of Jewish interactions. Possibly this is related to being the last European country to adopt monotheism and Christianity. Between 1095 and the 1500s the Crusaders rampaged across Europe, initially en route to the Holy Land in efforts to reclaim it from Muslim control for Christianity. Later, however, for various religious, economic, and political reasons, the crusaders waged havoc to all non-Catholics, and especially the Jews. Many Jews thus fled upon their approach, moving east to the relatively benign conditions that were present in Lithuania. This appears to be the start of The Litvak population.

In 1236, Mindaugas became king and united many of the Lithuanian tribes. For a while he converted to Christianity; however, he soon decided this was not for him and reverted to paganism. It took two hundred years before Christianity was fully established in the country.

Grand Duke Gediminas (1316–1341) fought against the Germanic Teutonic Knights and vastly expanded the country. He was a true visionary and invited all peoples to settle in the land. Many Jews came from Persia and Babylonia as well as Germany and France for the religious tolerance, tax exemptions, and land offered by Gediminas. His grandson, Grand Duke Vytautas (1392–1430), continued these tolerant attitudes. Under his leadership, Lithuania extended from the Black Sea in the East to the Baltic Sea in the West. Good conditions for Jews persisted in Lithuania for over two hundred years. Toward the mid-1500s, however, despite favorable Jewish laws, many of the lower nobility (predominantly middle class non-Jewish citizens) and Christian clergy began to intimidate the Jews. In some cases Jews were forced from the towns or degraded by having to wear yellow hats in public.

In 1569 the Grand Duchy of Lithuania and the Kingdom of Poland joined to form the Polish-Lithuanian Commonwealth, which persisted until 1795. Initially, again, Jews generally thrived, and tolerant laws remained in place. The Lithuanian nobility also prospered and adopted more and more of the Polish customs and traditions. They hired many Jews to run their estates and businesses, and especially to collect taxes. Furthermore, Jews were permitted to run taverns and make and sell alcohol—all under the aegis of the nobility. Naturally, this produced resentment by the villagers, serfs and peasants who only saw the prosperous face of these Jews. Generally, however, Jews continued to do well within The Commonwealth. Many poured into the country, especially following the Cossack massacres of 1648–1650 in the Ukraine, led by Chmielnicki (Chmiel the Wicked).

This then is the scene when our first Groidam/Graudan ancestor, Mana Groidam, makes his appearance around 1756—in the Polish-Lithuanian Commonwealth. The family may have come to Lithuania fleeing the crusaders or the Cossacks, or after having been expelled from Spain in 1492. Mana may have been born in a stetl (town); perhaps, even in Vilnius. By 1784 there were 5,000 Jews living in Vilnius. Shortly thereafter many were driven out of the city and moved west toward the Kaunas region, where Panevezys is situated. We do know that by 1834 his son Orel was fifty-three years old, and was established in Panevezys (Fig 2.2).

The late 1700s were turbulent times in the Commonwealth, which by now was starting to disintegrate. Mana would have been a teenager when Russia, together with Austria and Prussia, began dividing up the Polish Lithuanian Commonwealth (in 1772). By the time of the final dissolution in 1795, when the Grand Duchy of Lithuania became part of Czarist Russia under the Romanov Catherine the Great (Empress of Russia 1762–1796), he would have been in his mid-thirties with a fourteen-year-old son Orel Groidam (born about 1781). The family was probably well established in Panevezys, and there were 10,000 to 15,000 Jews living in what is now Lithuania.

Thus our earliest known ancestors, Mana Groidam and his son Orel, were born into the Polish-Lithuanian Commonwealth, which was generally characterized as being fairly benevolent toward the Jews. Under Czarist Russia, however, the situation changed dramatically. The Romanovs' instituted a policy of severe Russianization, and demanded support for the Russian Orthodox Church. People were expected to forgo their native languages and religions, speak Russian, teach and learn in Russian, and adopt Russian names, dress, and attitudes. For those who did not follow orders there was severe discrimination.

Of major significance is that during the latter part of the reign of Catherine II, "The Pale of Settlement" came into being. Prior to the absorption of the Commonwealth into Russia (1795), Jews had not been a significant population or influence in the Russian Empire. Now, all of a sudden, there was a massive increase. Not only that, but whereas Russian society had classically been divided into nobility, serfs, and clergy, at this time a middle class was developing and was largely being filled by Jews. In an attempt to develop a non-Jewish middle class in what may be termed "Old Russia" (that is, pre-1795), Catherine II established The Pale of Settlement. This corresponded more or less to the regions of the old Polish-Lithuanian Commonwealth, though its extent fluctuated over the years. Jews living within "The Pale" were forced to remain there. Various attempts were made to move Jews from "Old Russia" into The Pale. In other words, The Pale became the biggest ghetto in history, and remained in force from around 1791 to 1917. This was another part of the over-riding Russian policy to develop the empire as an assimilated Russian Orthodox Christian society.

Such was the prevailing atmosphere as Orel was growing into manhood. In 1796, when he was about fifteen, Empress Catherine II died and she was succeeded by her son Paul I (1796–1801), who vigorously pursued Russianization and discrimination. He reduced the authority of the Kahals, which were the local Jewish community councils responsible for managing Jewish affairs. Jews and Jewish businesses were taxed at double the level of Christians. In many of the Lithuanian villages, Jews formed forty to over 50 percent of the population. Our village, Panevezys, had a total population of 8,843 taxpayers, of which 5,836 were Jewish (per the Russian census, 1797).

The situation became even more difficult for Orel and the Groidam family in 1804 when a special Jewish statute was published. By now, Czar Paul I had been assassinated and was replaced by his son Alexander I (1801–1825). Orel was about twenty-three years of age. Jews from "Old Russia" were being forced into The Pale. They could no longer deal in alcohol, they were not allowed to run village inns, and they could not get any help to establish or maintain their businesses. By 1808 nearly half the Jewish labor force in The Pale was unemployed. Poverty was prevalent and competition intense. Possibly the Groidams, like so many other Jewish families, had to rely on welfare for some of their existence during this time.

In 1807, Orel may have seen some help coming for his family. After Napoleon's Prussian and Polish campaign, France occupied Lithuania and Jews were granted equality under the Napoleonic code. This was a brief respite, however; after the Treaty of Tilsit in 1808, Lithuania was handed back to the Russians. Alexander I raised taxes and, again, made it very difficult for the Jews.

When Orel was in his early thirties, in 1812, he was again exposed to Napoleonic influences. This time much closer to home, as the French army advanced through Lithuania toward to Moscow and then again six months later when they retreated in total disarray. On June 23, 1812, Napoleons' forces crossed the River Nemunas to enter Kaunas, about fifty miles South of Panevezys. By June 27, they controlled the capital Vilnius, where a provincial government for the Grand Duchy of Lithuania was established. One can only imagine the news as it percolated up to Panevezys. The period of June 23–27, 1812, was one of extreme heat and drought, and during the short march to Vilnius over 15,000 horses died and 50,000 of Napoleon's troops deserted. For the next five days violent thunderstorms and rain covered the country. Some Jews initially welcomed the French troops as liberators from Russian oppression; however, as conditions became worse, Napoleonic soldiers resorted to burning, plundering, stealing, and marauding. The extent to which this spread to Orel and his family in Panevezys is unknown. By this time he already had a four-year-old son Ovsey (Russianized version of Josiah). He was almost certainly aware of the Yiddish papers that soon circulated, urging Jews to support and pray for the Czar and his troops.

The final defeat of Napoleon, and the Congress of Vienna in 1815, left Lithuania once again as a part of the Russian Empire under Czar Alexander I, who initially tried to introduce more liberal ideas. Soon, however, the classic Russian policies of assimilation, indoctrination, and intimidation returned. The Graudans were exposed to the mass attempt to convert all Jews to Christianity (under Nicholas I), which obviously failed. At times Jews were forced to leave the smaller villages (stetls) and move into the towns such as Panevezys; however, when this did not work out, the law was changed. In 1825 when Alexander I died and was replaced by his younger brother Nicholas I (1825–1855), Ovsey would have been about seventeen years old and his father Orel would have been forty-four.

The family was now subjected to even more harassment. Nicholas I was a most unenlightened ruler; his reign was characterized by intense oppression and cruelty. In 1827, Jews in the nearby town of Telz, were accused of using blood of Christians to make matzah (unleavened bread for Passover)—the so-called blood libel. This resulted in new attacks and pogroms.

In the same year, The Committee for Jewish Affairs passed a far-reaching, iniquitous law: compulsory military service for Jews in Russia for a period of twenty-five years! Prior to this, Jews were not permitted into the Russian army (however, were taxed at a much higher rate). One can imagine the consternation this must have created in the Graudan household when Orel came home one evening. The news would have been that nineteen-year-old Ovsey had to leave the family and enter the army for what ostensibly could be the rest of his life. "Fortunately," he would have been too old to be forced to become a cantonist or "Nicholas soldier." By law, children between the ages of twelve and eighteen—but, in fact, many as young as eight to nine—were taken from their families and placed in special establishments (cantonal battalions), to "train" to become ready to enter the army at the age of eighteen, for their twenty-five-year conscription. The true aim, however, was to totally Russianize these children; to remove any attachments they had to Judaism and their families, and basically force them to convert to the Russian Orthodox Church. Once in the cantonments, they could not speak Yiddish, were forced to eat non-kosher food (or starve), were not allowed to pray, and were forced to attend Christian religious services. The majority, thus, succumbed and were soon converted and baptized. If they resisted, they died of a combination of disease, starvation, and over-work.

The Jewish population had to provide more than twice the number of conscripts than non-Jews: ten out of every one thousand males annually in every draft, as opposed to seven out of one thousand every second year. Local Jewish councils, the Kahals, were given the responsibility of providing the recruits. Many times they employed unscrupulous Jews to kidnap children, usually the poor, and have them sent off to their terror and largely their doom. These, in Yiddish, were descriptively called the khappers (grabbers).

Somehow it seems Ovsey avoided the draft. The family was probably fairly well off and managed to buy or bribe their way out. Maybe Mana paid a poor neighbor to send their son instead of Ovsey. The Graudans could have been special craftsmen, factory workers, or members of one of the merchant guilds. They would have, therefore, been exempt from a draft. It is doubtful they were Rabbi's. Another possibility is that Ovsey attended a non-Jewish school, was the eldest son, ran away, and hid for many years; then changed his name, or even mutilated himself. All of these ploys were, in fact, used by Jews of the time to avoid the interminable sentence. This 1827 law enforcing Jewish conscription into the Russian army was to be one of the major stimulants for Jews to flee Russia and emigrate during the mid- to late 1800s.

We know from the revised census that by April 20, 1834, Ovsey was married to Sheine and they had a seven-year-old daughter Khave. Their son Israel was probably a newborn, and so would not have been included in the census. Although the census states his name as Govsei and records his age as twenty-three, this is probably incorrect. Such errors represent the marked inaccuracies of the time. From his death record he would have been around twenty-seven years old, which is more likely.

The following year, in 1835, the life of Ovsey and his young family became even harsher. Czar Nicholas passed the statute for Regulation of Jewish Affairs. Jews were expelled from villages and, especially a few years later, from those villages within thirty-five miles of the German and Austrian borders. This resulted in more Jews coming into the larger towns such as Panevezys, which were already overcrowded, but only a few Jews being able to make any kind of living to support their families.

Ten years later, in 1844, when Ovsey was in his thirties with teenage daughter Khave and son Israel, almost bar mitzvah age, legislation was passed that further decreased any autonomy Jews might have had. The Jewish community councils, the Kahals, were abolished. Their functions were largely taken over by the state; except the conscription quotas and tax collections—these were done by state-appointed Jews, and in many cases the job went to the highest Jewish bidder. The most offensive of these was the hated Basket Tax. Thus a Jewish friend, neighbor, or family member may well have come to the Graudans to collect the taxes, or it could have been the other way around!

The Basket Tax included trade licenses and a tax on clothing, including men's skull caps (caftans or yarmulkes) and women's wigs (sheitals). The tax for wearing a yarmulke was five rubles. These clothing taxes and restrictions were only imposed on Jews. Mohammedans and heathens were allowed to wear any clothing they liked. The Box (or "Korobka") Tax was a special part of the Basket Tax. This was imposed on every animal killed according to Jewish law (Kashrut) and then again when the meat was sold at the market. Another tax was the Candle Tax, imposed on Sabbath candles. All of this must have led to many heated a discussion in the Graudan home.

Ovsey and Sheine must really have thought some help was on the way when they heard the news in 1846 that the very rich and famous English Jew Sir Moses Monteifiore was visiting Czar Nicholas. Sir Moses was welcomed with much pomp and celebration. He also visited nearby towns, including Kaunas and Ukmerge, where speeches were made and discussions were held. Sadly, Ovsey would have soon realized that this visit would do nothing to improve his lot. Czar Nicholas even responded a few months later by issuing an order to forbid men from wearing sidelocks (peyes). Ovsey would have heard reports and probably saw the police publicly shaving off young men's peyes.

Further fear and oppression came to Ovsey, Sheine, and Israel in 1854. At this time, Czar Nicholas I provoked the Ottoman Turks to remove the French and the Roman Catholic Church from controlling the holy sites in Jerusalem. Nicholas also wanted to expand Russia at the expense of the declining Ottoman Empire. Eventually, Britain and France declared War on Russia in March 1854, and thus started the Crimean War (1854–1856). Nicholas then needed more soldiers and resources from his citizens. Somehow it would appear that, once again, the Graudans in Panevezys managed to avoid having a son conscripted for a terrible war. Twenty-year-old Israel Graudan was certainly of military age, however he survived this stressful period in Russia's history. At an early age about this time and probably during the War, Israel married Hinda Etta Sieff in Panevezys. He was around twenty-one years old and she was twenty. This may well have been the reason he managed to avoid conscription. Shortly after the end of the war in c. 1856 my great-grandmother Johanna was born. Within a few years after her birth, the son Moritz was born, and then the second daughter Rocha was born (1861).

This very dark period for Jews in the Russian Empire came to an end in 1855 when Czar Nicholas I died during the course of the Crimean War. For Jews, his reign had been one of the most dreadful in Russian history, especially in view of the "Nicholas Soldiers," and the twenty-five-year conscription that Nicholas had introduced in 1827. By placing the responsibility on the Jews themselves to provide the required numbers, this had not only pitted non-Jews against the Jews, but it had stirred up Jewish-Jewish hatreds.

Israel and Hinda Etta would have been particularly encouraged early on in their marriage when Alexander II replaced his father Nicholas I as Czar of Russia. They were likely very surprised when at his coronation in Moscow in 1855, Czar Alexander II announced that Jews would be conscripted into the army on equal terms with non-Jews. Russia was thoroughly defeated in the Crimean War; yet, initially Alexander II continued with his reforms such that he came to be called "The Liberator." The cantonal decree was abolished, thus putting an end to the kidnapping of children, an act particularly significant to Israel and Hinda Etta with their young family. And military service was reduced from twenty-five to sixteen years.

In 1859 a proclamation from the Czar permitted some Jews to leave The Pale and settle anywhere within the Russian Empire. University-educated Jews, those working as skilled manual workers, merchants, and distillers were allowed to avail themselves of this new law. Despite this liberalization in the land, and the hopes pinned on the latest Czar, conditions were still appalling for most Jews in Russia, and especially those within The Pale. Unemployment, hunger, and overcrowding were rife. Around 40 percent of Jewish families received welfare assistance from overseas.

These then may have been the factors that encouraged and enabled Israel, Hinda Etta, and their young family to move the fairly short distance from Panevezys in Lithuania, which was within The Pale, across the border to beautiful Libau in Latvia, which was Beyond the Pale. Maybe it was the Great Famine of 1867 in Lithuania or the Cholera Epidemic of 1868 that was the final precipitating factor. Of course, in order to move away from The Pale required the family to have approval from the Russian Government which may have been sanctioned due to Israel's work. By this time, he was a corn trader which would have given him the freedom to move. The death of their fifteen-year-old son, Nicholas, must have added to Israel and Hinda Etta's unhappy feelings about leaving the land of their birth. Nevertheless, sometime between 1861 and 1878 they said goodbye to Israel's parents Ovsey and Sheine, and they moved to Libau. In 1878, Ovsey died in Panevezys and Sheine died in 1882. Both were buried in the Panevezys Jewish Cemetery. As this was not too far away, Israel and Hinda Etta may have even attended the funerals.

* * *

From 2007 to 2009, I (Keith) was involved in a project to build a memorial to the Jewish Cemetery in Panevezys, which had been totally destroyed by the soviets in 1966. The Headstones had been used for building roads and walls! This "Memorial to a Grieving Jewish Mother" opened in Panevezys on September 24, 2009. Ovsey and Sheine Graudan are commemorated on this memorial (Figs. 3.1 and 3.2).

Figure 3.1 Valda, Jessica, and Keith at Opening of Grieving Jewish Mother Memorial to the Cemetery in Panevezys, Lithuania. 24 September 2009

RĖMĖJAI

PANEVĖŽIO MIESTO SAVIVALDYBĖ, LIETUVOS ŽYDŲ BENDRUOMENĖ, PANEVĖŽIO MIESTO ŽYDŲ BENDRUOMENĖ, IZRAELIO AMBASADA, RUSIJOS FEDERACIJOS AMBASADA, AMERIKOS FONDAS LIETUVOS IR LATVIJOS ŽYDAMS, PANEVĖŽIO GYVOJO DIEVO KRIKŠČIONIŲ BAŽNYČIA,

HOWARD MARGOL, ESTHER MARGOL, JURIJ GRAFMAN, SVETLANA GRAFMAN, DR. KEITH KAYE, VALDA KAYE, JESSICA M. KAYE, DEBORAH R. KAYE, MAXINE J. KAYE, REA GARDY, MICHAEL LEVY, STEPHANIE LEVY, DR. CHARLES B. NAM, MARTIN SCHAFFEL, DR DAN JACOBS, JANICE JACOBS,

DR. SIMONAS ALPERAVIČIUS, MARGARITA GUREVIČIENĖ, SIMONAS GUREVIČIUS, ARTURAS TAICAS, MICHAILAS GRAFMANAS, JURIJUS SMIRNOVAS, ZINAIDA ZAPRUDSKAJA, NADEŽDA SEDYCH, GENNADY KOFMAN, VALENTINA DARENCEVA, RASHELLE VOVSY, JEANNE STUTMAN

Kaye šeima paramą skyrė mirusių Owsey Graudan (1808–1878), Sheinos Graudan (1796–1882), Malkos Zhiv (1823–1895), Biniamino Kaplanovski (1815–1890), Eigos Kaplanovski (1814 – 1887), Khaios Kaplanovski (mirė 1882 m.), Rashos Kaplanovski (1860–1902) atminimui

Figure 3.2. Back of Grieving Jewish Mother Memorial with inscribed names of Owsey and Sheine Graudan together with other Kaye (Kaplan) Family Members

CHAPTER 4

Move to Latvia
(2nd Great-Grandparents)

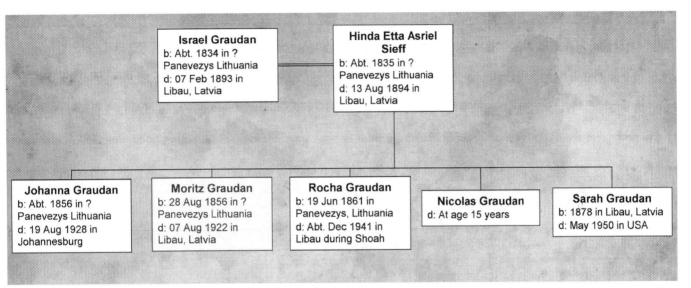

Figure 4.1. Children of Israel Graudan and Hinda Etta Sieff. The founding siblings

Israel Graudan (born abt 1834) and wife Hinda Etta Sieff (born abt 1835)

Author's 2nd great-grandparents (great-great-grandparents).

Israel was probably born in Panevezys around 1834 and Hinda Etta about 1835. Between 1861 and 1878 Israel, Hinda, and at least three of their five children left Panevezys, Lithuania, and moved to Libau, Latvia. We know their second daughter Rocha was born in Panevezys in 1861. Presumably, therefore, the two elder children, Johanna and Moritz, were also born in Panevezys. One child, Nicolas, died at age fifteen. We are not sure where. The youngest daughter Sarah was born in Libau in 1878. We also know, from the Latvian Archive Records, that Israel worked as a corn trader in Libau, and that in 1886 he and his wife, Hinda Etta, were living at Schiffer (Kugu) Street in the house of Sachs. He had no property and died in Libau on February 7, 1893, of emphysema.

There are three records for Israel.

1. Family List 1908 of Panevezys Jewish Community.

Again, for some reason Israel, his wife, and five children are documented in the Family List 1908 of Panevezys Jewish Community despite the fact that they had moved from there many years previously. Certainly their names and ages correlate completely. "Graudan Izrel ben Ovsei seventy-four years old and his wife Ginda-Eta seventy-four years old. His children: Movsha-Itsyk forty-nine years old, Khana fifty-two years old, Rakhel forty-six years old, and Sora thirty-seven years old."

2. Latvian State Archives: List of Jewish Families Originated Not from Courland but Living in Libau, set up in 1889, 1893, and 1896. "Israil (Israel, Asriel) son of Owsey Graudan from Ponevezh" (Fig. 4.2).

3. Libau Jewish Community Death Records for 1893 (Fig. 4.3).

№ по порядку	Званіе, имя, отчество и фамилія.	Семейное положеніе.	Срокъ обязатель-наго выѣзда.	Родъ занятія.	ПРИМѢЧАНІЕ.

The list of the Jewish families, originated not from Courland, but living in Libau, set up in ca 1893:

Nr. 21
Ponevezh petty bourgeois Israel, son of Owsey Grauden (sic). Occupation – without occupation.
His wife Hinda, daughter of Abel (maiden name is not stated), aged 55,
Children:
- Rocha, aged 19,
- Sore, aged 17.

Israel Grauden lived in Libau more then 10 years, since 1878. He had no property.

KOPIJA PAREIZA
96
1/63
LVVA direktore
izpildītājs
200_g.

Figure 4.2. From Latvian Archives showing that Israel Graudan, his wife Hinda and children Rocha and Sore had come to Latvia from Panevezys in or before 1878. Above, Original Russian. Below, Official Translation

№		Гдѣ умеръ и погребенъ.	Число и Мѣсяцъ.		Лѣта.	Болѣзнь, или отъ чего умеръ.	Кто умеръ.
Женскаго.	Мужескаго.		Христіанскій.	Еврейскій.			
	9	Въ Либавѣ (гор. Либавъ)	5 фев.	19 адар	74 года	отъ всеобщей слабости	Ковенскій мѣщанинъ Иценъ Александровъ Израельсонъ
	10	"	7 фев. 3 адар	59 минут	отъ эмфиземы легкихъ	Поневѣжскій мѣщанинъ Израиль Овсеевичъ Граубартъ

מספר | | | | | | |

| מי מת ובזה שמה ומעמדה . או | מזה שמה ומה היתה בתולה | או נשואה או אלמנה | ממה המות מחלי או | מסיבה אחרת | כמה שני המת | חודש ויום המיתה | | | | באיזה עיר מת ונקבר | מספר |

Appendix No. 6

The death registration entry no. 10 in the death records of the Jewish community in Libau for 1893.

Ponevezh petty bourgeois Israel, son of Owsey Graudan died on February 7 of 1893 (Julian calendar) in Libau, aged 59, cause of death — emphysema of the lungs

Figure 4.3. Israel Graudan Death Record (#10) from Death Records of Libau Jewish community 1893. Top in Russian; Middle, Yiddish using Hebrew Script; Below Official Translation

Hinda Etta Sieff (born abt 1835, probably in Panevezys)

She died in Libau on August 13, 1894, at age fifty-nine from gullet cancer. Her parents were Abel Zhif (Sieff) and Malka.

There are three records for Hinda Etta.

1. Family List 1908 of Panevezys Jewish Community

2. Latvian State Archives List of Jewish Families Originated Not from Courland but Living in Libau, (Fig. 4.2).

3. Libau Jewish Community Death Records for 1894. (Fig. 4.4).

Appendix No. 7

The death registration entry No. 23 in the death records of the Jewish Community in Libau for 1894:

Ponevezh petty bourgeois, a widow Hinda-Eta Asriel Graudan, died on August 13 of 1894 (Julian calendar) aged 59, cause of death – gullet cancer.

Figure 4.4. Death Record #23 for Libau Jewish Community 1894

CHAPTER 5

Latvian Jews and the Graudan Family in Libau

Liepāja is situated on the Baltic coast in the southern part of Latvia about 60 km north of Lithuania (Fig. 5.1). It is perched on a narrow strip of land about 2 km wide, with the Baltic Ocean on the west and Liepāja Lake on the east. The lake is 2–3 km wide, about 15 km long and toward its north side it is connected to the ocean by a dredged-out canal, which is the Liepāja Harbor (Fig. 5.7).

Figure 5.1. Map of The Baltic

The city started as a fishing village around the thirteenth century. The river and village of Liva were first mentioned in writings from 1253. One of the suggested origins of the name was the word liiv from the old Estonian language, meaning "sand." This is most appropriate in view of the miles-long, beautiful sandy beach (Figs. 5.2, 5.3).

Figure 5.2. Beach at Liepaja 2007

Figure 5.3. Exploring the beach

The coat of arms of Libau has a linden tree with a red lion leaning against it (Fig. 5.4). Prior to 1562, Latvia was ruled by German knightly orders, which totally banned all Jews. This was not the case with neighboring Lithuania, which had a Jewish population from the 1200s.

The first Jews appear to have come into southern Latvia, to an area known as Kurland (Courland). By 1562, Kurland was a semi-independent duchy ruled by Duke Magnuss, brother of the King of Denmark. Jews first seem to have entered Kurland as merchants around 1571, probably from Prussia. From the earliest times therefore, these Jews were more German-Jewish than the Yiddish-speaking Lithuanian Jews. The significance of Kurland lies in the important, all-season trading harbors of Libau and Windau; the harbor of Riga, the largest Latvian city, was closed in the winter (Fig. 5.5).

Figure 5.4. Keith at entrance to Liepaja, 2007

Figure 5.5. Libau Harbor lined by buildings that used to be herring warehouses

In the 1700s many skilled Jewish workers and artisans arrived in Kurland from Germany. The first synagogue was built in Aizpute (Hasenpoth) in 1708. Until 1717, there were no taxes imposed on Jews. The German way of life thus dominated Jews in Kurland, with German (not Yiddish) being the most common spoken language of the Jewish community. This continued until World War II.

In 1795 Kurland, like Lithuania and the rest of Latvia, became part of the Russian Empire and remained so until 1918. It was not part of the Pale of Settlement. Despite this, however, a few years after becoming a part of the Russian Empire, the Russian Emperor Paul promulgated a law entitling those Jews already in Kurland to have legal status as permanent inhabitants. This, at a cost of double taxation! However, this did enable Kurland Jews to take part in local government elections and encouraged their integration into German society. By 1850 there was a secular Jewish School in Libau, in addition to religious schools (Talmud Torahs). There were 23,743 Jews documented in Kurland in 1852. The all-of-Russia census of 1897 documented 51,072 Jews living in Kurland.

There were many difficulties in the Pale of Settlement, and some Jews managed to leave. From the records, Israel Graudan, his wife Hinda Etta, and their three children, Johanna, Moritz, and Rocha, left Panevezys, Lithuania, and went to Libau between 1861 and 1878 (Fig. 4.2). This must have been an exciting move for the young family. Assuming it was 1870, Israel would have been thirty-six, Johanna about fifteen, Moritz fourteen, and Rocha nine. They already had one tragedy with the death of fifteen-year-old Nicolas, who remained behind, buried with his ancestors in the Panevezys Cemetery. A new beginning in a new land started with Sarah. The first Graudan to be born in the promising, beautiful seaside city of Libau, Sarah was born in 1878, not long after the move.

Leaving behind The Pale and coming to Libau must have been a great relief for Israel and his family compared to the difficulties and overcrowding of Panevezys. The children could go to school and in the summer play on the magnificent beach. During most of the time in Czarist Russia the Jews of Libau led a fairly comfortable life of liberal tolerance. Many of these newer Jewish immigrants probably initially spoke Yiddish, rather than the German spoken by older, established Libau Jews; and, certainly, the newcomers would have been looked down upon by the elite, cultured, and established, German-speaking Jews. However, we know—both from her granddaughter Ruth Levine and from her diary—that Sarah Graudan spoke High German (Hoch Deutsch) and also had the usual, somewhat superior, attitude toward Yiddish. Possibly German had been the Graudan home language from Panevezys times, or perhaps Sarah had gone to a German School in Libau.

Arriving in Latvia in the 1870s, the Graudans were under the rule of Russian Czar Alexander II (The Liberator), who had started his reign with much liberal gusto. By this time, however, after an 1866 assassination attempt on his life, Alexander II had lost some of this luster. He was assassinated in 1881 and replaced by his son Alexander III, who soon came to repudiate many of his father's advances. The May Laws of 1882 prohibited Jews from doing business on Sundays and Christian Holidays, and from buying property; and the Commission on the Jewish Question, established in 1883, spent five years deliberating and then coming up with six hundred and fifty laws specifically affecting the rights and freedoms of Russian Jews. Also, by the 1890s Russianization was very prominent and the Russian language was mandatory. The Jewish problem was prophesized by the Rusian State to be resolved by one-third Jews being forced to emigrate, one-third baptized, and the remainder starved to death.

By this point in the 1890s, the four Graudan children, Johanna, Moritz, Rocha, and Sarah, had grown up in Libau. Johanna was married to Julius Holzberg and already had four children: Minna (b. 1979), Rebecca (b. 1879), Theodore (b. 1882), and Isay-Kalman (b. 1884). Moritz and Rocha were probably married but as of yet without children. The youngest, Libau-born Sarah would have been nineteen years old. The life experienced by the Graudan families in Libau seems to have been generally pleasant despite increasingly severe laws, as has been so well described by the writings of Robert Herzenberg (Appendix 1).

With great foresight, Johanna and Julius Holzberg took advantage of the Russian government policy of encouraging Jewish emigration. Sometime in the 1890s they moved their whole family to South Africa; thus, for a second time Johanna changed countries (the first time was when she was a teenager, when she moved from Lithuania to Latvia). When she moved to South Africa she was a married woman with four children.

Moritz, Rocha, and Sarah remained in Libau. They experienced the death of Czar Alexander III at age fifty in 1894, and his replacement, the last Czar, Nicholas II (1894–1917). In 1912, Sarah and her husband Isaac Quasser and their two children Adolph and Judith left Libau for the United States. By 1914 there were ten thousand Jews in Libau (out of a population of 119,000) and about 25 percent of all industry was in Jewish hands.

Moritz lived through The Russian Revolution to die in Libau in 1922. An idea of the Jewish lifestyle in Libau in the 1920s can be seen through the eyes of Sarah, from her account of the time she visited her family on a trip from Ohio in 1928 (Appendix 2). Rocha married Samuel Friedlander in Libau and they had three daughters, Dina, Jenny, and Henriette. Although Samuel died before the Second World War, Rocha, Dina, and Jenny suffered the full consequences of The Holocaust (Appendix 3). Henriette married Sima Linkovski shortly before the Russian Revolution of 1917 and through great bravery and foresight managed to obtain French citizenship; she survived the war.

* * *

When I (Keith) visited Liepāja in the summer of 2007, the remnants of its former glory as a major seaport and holiday resort could still be seen. Nestled as it is between the Baltic Sea on the west and the marshy Liepāja Lake on the east, many streets still consisted of what once were magnificent wooden homes (Fig. 5.6). I was particularly excited to find Uliha Street, and especially Uliha Street #11 (Fig. 5.7, 5.8, 5.9). How glorious this must have been before the Second World War. Rocha and Jenny lived on the top floor in apartment #6. There home was only a short walk up the road and across the park to the never-ending white sandy beach. Wonderful times they must have had.

Now however, after a rainy gray morning, all was sad. All that was left was a dilapidated building with peeled paint, raw wounds of dissolving wood and concrete, and an irregular creaking stairway up to the battered door of apartment #6. This was as far as I got.

Figure 5.6. Intricately-carved verandah on old wooden Liepaja home

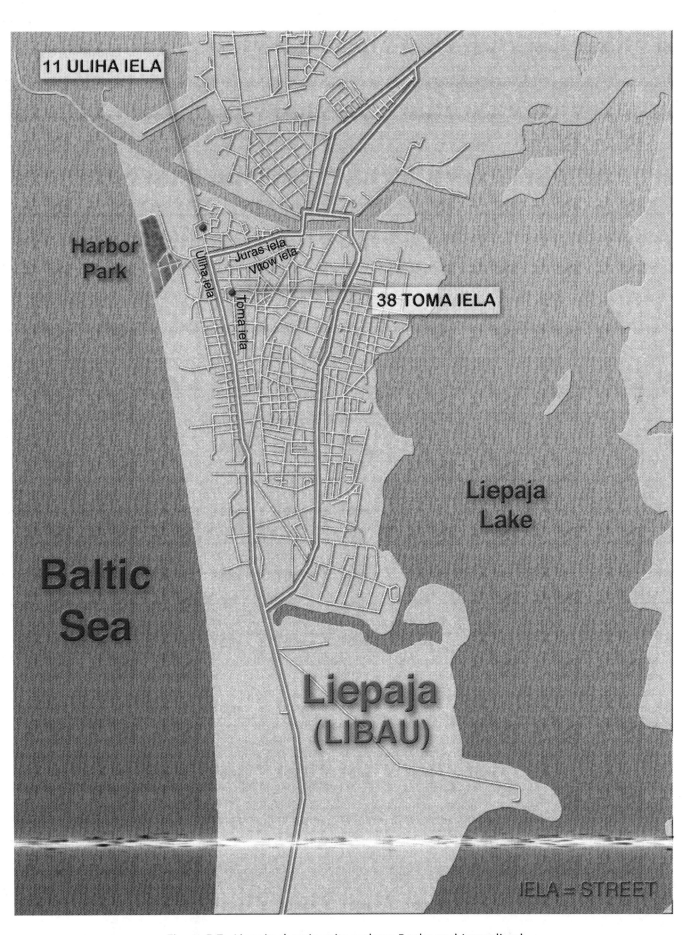

11 ULIHA IELA

Harbor
Park

Juras iela
Vitow iela

Uliha iela

Toma iela

38 TOMA IELA

Liepaja
Lake

Baltic
Sea

Liepaja
(LIBAU)

IELA = STREET

Figure 5.7. Liepaja showing sites where Rocha and Jenny lived

27

Figure 5.8. 11 Uliha Street, Libau; top floor is apartment #6,
where Rocha and Jenny lived before The Second World War

Figure 5.9. The wounds of war and sovietization. (Keith, 2007)

From here, I took another short, exciting, emotionally-draining walk to 38 Toma Street. Apartment #3 was on the first floor. This was almost certainly the place from where Rocha and Jenny were taken to their doom (Fig. 5.10).

Figure 5.10. 38 Toma Street. Apartment #3 is the top four windows

CHAPTER 6

South African Graudans
(Johanna and Her Descendents)

The Founding Couple

Figure 6.1. **Johanna Graudan**
b: c. 1856, Probably Panevezys, Lithuania;
d: 19 Aug 1928, Jhb, S. Africa;

Figure 6.2. **Julius Holzberg**
b: c. 1854, Probably Salanty, Lithuania
d: 28 Jun 1926, Vrede, S. Africa

* * *

Children
Children of Johanna Graudan and Julius Holzberg (n=4):

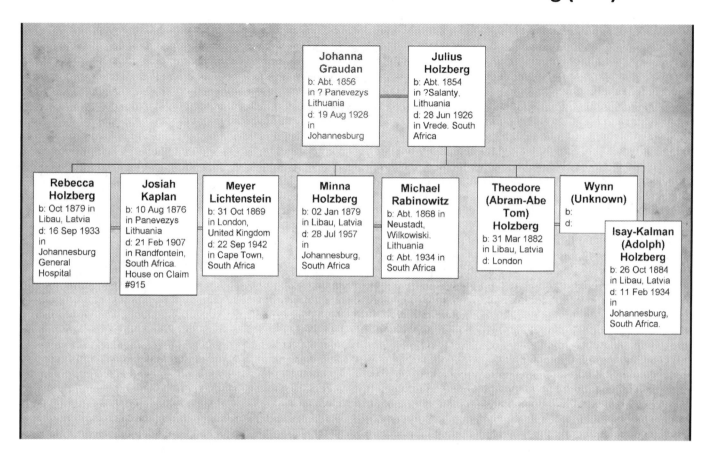

Figure 6.3. Children of Johanna Graudan and Julius Holzberg

1. Holzberg, **Minna**

b: 2 Jan. 1879, Libau, Latvia
d: 28 July 1957, Johannesburg, S. Africa
m: Michael Rabinowitz (Buhai), c. 1903, S. Africa

Figure 6.4.

2. Holzberg, **Rebecca**

b: Oct. 1879, Libau, Latvia
d: 16 Sept. 1933 Johannesburg, S. Africa
m: Josiah Kaplan (Ovsei Kaplanovski), c. 1905, S. Africa
m: Meyer Lichtenstein, c. 1910, S. Africa

Figure 6.5.

Memories

As told by Josse to his son Keith.

Moved to S. Africa with her parents c. 1890. Married Josiah Kaplan (b. Panevezys, Lithuania) in S. Africa. Josiah, a commercial traveler, died from fish poisoning just five days after Josse was born in Randfontein, near Johannesburg. Two years later she married Meyer Lichtenstein (b. London) who had children from a previous marriage. Died in her son Josse's arms at Johannesburg (Jhb) Hospital when a drain was removed following a cholecystectomy.

3. Holzberg, **Theodore (Abram-Abe, Tom Holt)**

b: 31 March 1882, Libau, Latvia
d: London, UK
m: Wynn

Figure 6.6.

Memories

By Keith

Was fondly called Uncle Tom by Josse. Changed his name to Tom Holt. Lived in London with his wife Wynn. Was very friendly with Josse and Helga. Wrote a small red book, which Keith remembers in Josse's library in Bryanston, Jhb. They had no children.

4. Holzberg, **Adolph (Isay-Kalman)**

b: 26 Oct. 1884, Libau, Latvia
d: 11 Feb. 1934, Johannesburg, S. Africa

Figure 6.7.

* * *

Grandchildren

Grandchildren of Johanna Graudan and Julius Holzberg (n=11):
Minna Holzberg Family (n=6)

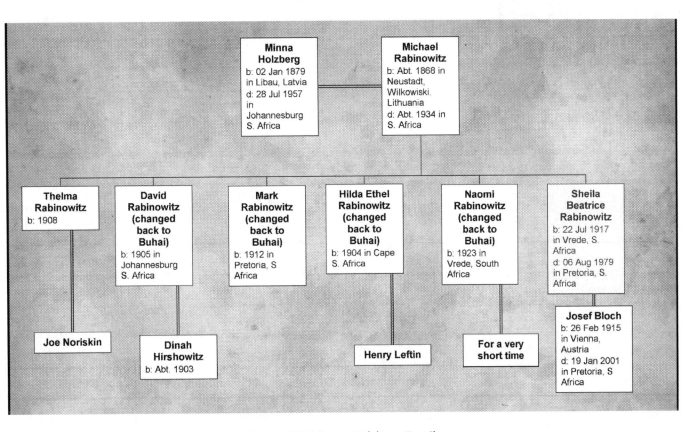

Figure 6.8 Minna Holzberg Family

1. Rabinowitz, **Hilda Ethel (Buhai)**

b: 1904, Cape, S. Africa
d: S. Africa
m: Henry Leftin

Figure 6.9.

2. Rabinowitz, **David (Buhai)**

b: 1905, Johannesburg, S. Africa
d: S. Africa
m: Dinah Hirshowitz

Figure 6.10.

Memories

As told to Keith by Roger Buhai

David's father, Michael, was born as Michael Buhai in Lithuania. His grandfather was Moise Aaron Buhai and grandmother was Cherna Rabinowitz. In order to escape conscription into the Russian army, Michael changed his name to that of his mother's maiden name; i.e., Rabinowitz. He came to South Africa as Michael Rabinowitz and married Minna Holzberg; they were married as Michael and Minna Rabinowitz. On his deathbed, he asked his children to change their names back to Buhai. Thelma was already married to Joe Noriskin and so did not change her name; Hilda, David, Mark, and Naomi did change their names back to Buhai. Sheila did not change her name, as she was at University on a bursary and this would have been too complicated. Told to Roger Buhai by his father David and corroborated by Julia Kallmeyer (Sheila's daughter).

David was thus born as David Rabinowitz. He went to school and was in the South African army, Transvaal Scottish Division, under this name. He fought in the Second World War and was taken Prisoner of War. It was after the war that he changed back to Buhai. Keith remembers his father Josse saying that he and David were very close friends (first cousins). As young men growing up they spent lots of good times together on Michael and Minnie Rabinowitz's farm near Vrede in the "orange-free state."

3. Rabinowitz, **Thelma**

b: 1908, S. Africa
d: c. 1989 Johannesburg, S. Africa
m: Joseph Noriskin
occ: Chief Welfare Officer, Jewish Medical Council

Figure 6.11.

Memories

By Grandson Ian Goldman and Keith Kaye

Thelma lived in Vrede in her early years where her parents had a hotel. She was a tall and gangly woman—5'10" tall; and much taller than her husband Joe. She had a first degree in classics when she was eighteen, around 1926, which was very unusual at that time. She later achieved a degree in sociology and became a social worker, working in Sophiatown. It was here where she met and worked with Father Trevor Huddleston, the much loved priest and anti-apartheid activist. She had two children: Andra, and five years later Michael. Thelma and Joe lived on a beautiful estate in Morningside called Little Place off Outspan Road (which still exists), which was then in the country, outside of Johannesburg.

Keith remembers often going there for drives on a Sunday with Josse, Helga, and Rea. They had a wonderful tennis court at the bottom of the garden where the adults and sometimes Keith played. They also had horses, and Andra and Joe used to ride a lot. She wasn't an easy mother, and Andra and Michael didn't have an easy relationship with her, but she was a lovely granny. Ian called her "Cookie," because she called him that. Soon the name stuck, and everyone called her Cookie! She loved reading; she read a lot to her grandchildren. We developed our love of Greek myths from her. She also loved gardening, whether at Little Place or the flat they lived in in Winstead Gardens, where she specialized in growing Busy Lizzies and fuschias.

She lived long enough to know her first great-grandchildren, and we had a lovely holiday with her and Joe playing with Anna and Maya in the park next to Winstead Gardens. They finally moved to an old-age home about 1988, and Cookie didn't live long afterwards, while Joe outlived her by three to four years.

4. Rabinowitz, **Mark (Buhai)**

b: 1912, Pretoria, S. Africa
d: S. Africa

Figure 6.12.

Memories

By Keith

Mark was pretty much a loner. Never married. Always very nice and polite. At family functions would be quietly talking with the family and smoking his pipe.

5. Rabinowitz, **Sheila Beatrice**

b: 22 July 1917, Vrede, S. Africa
d: 6 Aug. 1979, Pretoria, S. Africa
m: Joseph Bloch

Figure 6.13.

Memories

By Keith

Sheila was a delight. Invariably with a warm, gracious smile. It was always a thrill when my dad would say on a Sunday, "Let's go for a drive to Pretoria to visit Sheila and Joe." They were the ultimate warm, welcoming couple.

6. Rabinowitz, **Naomi (Buhai)**

b: 1923, Vrede, S. Africa
d: S. Africa
m: For a short time to a sailor in Durban

Figure 6.14.

Grandchildren of Johanna Graudan and Julius Holzberg (n=11):
Rebecca Holzberg Family (n=5)

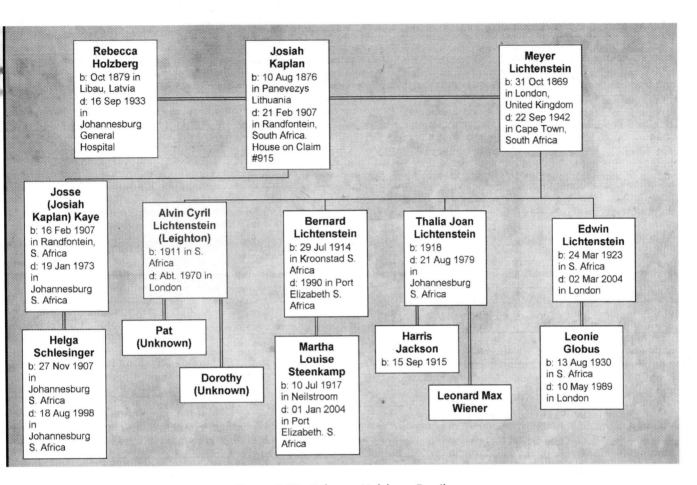

Figure 6.15. Rebecca Holzberg Family

1. Kaye, **Josse (Josiah Kaplan)**

b: 16 Feb. 1907, Randfontein, S. Africa
d: 19 Jan. 1973, Johannesburg. S. Africa
m: Helga Schlesinger, 19 June 1932, Johannesburg, S. Africa
occ: Professor of Radiology (U. Witwatersrand), Pharmacist, Optician
rec: Oil Painting, photography, cacti, cars, lawn bowls, archaeology

Figure 6.16.

Memories

By son Keith

When my dad died in Jhb General Hospital, where he had been Professor of Radiology, Drs. Barlow and Bothwell were outside his room. He was having difficulty breathing, as he had been since we rushed him to the hospital several days before. They asked Mom (Helga) to wait outside. A nurse went in to give a shot. I suspect this may have been morphine. The nurse called out. When Mom rushed in, Josse was partially out of bed. I think he was trying to stand up. Then he died. Earlier that day he had asked me to shave him, which I did. He had never asked me to do this before. I then went back to the hospital to clerk a new patient and at the exact time he died my hand started to shake uncontrollably. Although I did not know it at that stage, that was the moment of his death. I also knew that he had told me previously that he never, ever wanted to be a burden on anyone.

Shortly after he died, I (a registrar) was talking with one of the senior nephrologists on the street just below the beautiful gardens that were part of the Johannesburg General Hospital. Somehow we were talking about looks, when I said, "I've been told I look like my dad."

"Oh no!" he said, "Your father was *so* good looking!"

Found by Daughter Rea, January 2006.
Written by Josse at Rea's Birth.

Dad's tribute to his mom.

24.11.1933

My baby is born, and Helga was marvelous.

Rea June Kaye.

In the midst of my happiness, my life is tinged with a tragic loneliness and sorrow.

My mummy is re-born and with God's help I shall devote my life to the happiness of my wife and baby, as my mother devoted her life to mine.

28.11.33.

My baby was registered today and named after my mother, Rea June Kaye.

I would have her grow up as a monument to my mum and as a replica of her.

She must have mum's high laughing courage and infinite pluck, her impulsive generosity, her extravagant fastidiousness, her large-minded sympathy, and utter lack of pettiness and merce-nariness. She must be as comforting, consoling, and understanding; she must be able to laugh at herself and at circumstances; and she never, never take herself seriously; but any injustice, any hurt inflicted on another, must be able to move her to anger and pity.

She must be extravagant in thought, gracious, gay, and generous.

She must hate arrogance; browbeat meanness of thought or actions.

She must learn to love good living, to accept nothing shabby or second rate, but never to despise or misjudge poverty.

She must be satisfied with nothing but the best, she must learn to laugh at life and never to be afraid.

2. Leighton, **Alvin Cyril (Lichtenstein)**

b: 1911, S. Africa
d: c. 1970, London, UK
m: Pat (Died)
m: Doroth
occ: Lawyer

Figure 6.17.

Memories

By Keith

I adored my Uncles Alvin and Beck. When I was fifteen, in 1957, I represented S. Africa at the Jubilee Scout Jamboree in the UK. I well remember my first big trip into London from our campsite at Gilwell Park, just outside the city. Kalie Schiel (from Windhoek) and I, both in our Boy Scout uniforms, sat on the top of a red, double-decker London bus. We passed a large river, and I can still see the pitying look I got from the passenger next to me when I asked if this was The Thames. What could this be—The Nile? Eventually we arrived, unexpected and unannounced, at 2 Elm Park Gardens, a townhouse opposite a park in Chelsea. Alvin's wife Dorothy—a thin, tall, somewhat austere Englishwoman—took one look at us and said, "Alvin is at work. You didn't tell me you were coming. I have nothing for you to eat." So after our big adventure to get there, Kalie and I walked around the corner, had a sandwich in the local tea room, and spoke about the differences between English and S. African hospitality. In South Africa we would have been invited in immediately and given some tea and dry biscuits, if that was all there was in the house; and then afterwards we would have gone out to get something.

Anyways, things improved significantly after that and I ended up spending three weeks with Uncle Al and Dorothy. We had many a discussion about living in London versus South Africa. Alvin spoke about having to prove himself and was pretty chuffed when I said, "Well you are now a Professor at London School of Economics (I think it was LSE), so you have proven yourself. Now you can come back to your family in South Africa." He never did.

3. Leyton, **Bernard (Lichtenstein)**

b: 29 July 1914, Kroonstad, S. Africa
d: 6 Sept. 1996, Port Elizabeth . S. Africa
m: Martha Louise Steenkamp, 19 June 1932, Jhb, S. Africa
occ: Printer
rec: Lawn bowls, photography

Figure 6.18.

Memories

By Keith

I always enjoyed going to visit my Uncle Beck. I remember as a ten-year-old going with my dad and Uncle Beck to visit my sister Rea in Potchefstroom, and especially to take photographs, which the three of us so enjoyed. Those photographs still adorn the front of my first photo album.

4. Lichtenstein, **Thalia Joan**

b: 1918, S. Africa
d: 21 Aug. 1979, Johannesburg. S. Africa
m: Harris Jackson (divorced)
m: Leonard Max Weiner

Figure 6.19.

Memories

By Daughter Merril

Thalia was a ballerina in her youth and loved music and theatre. I remember her organizing plays at our school, and her advising my schoolmates on acting. She was completely displaced in South Africa, which was culturally isolated at that time, having no TV as a platform for exchange of ideas on art and being censored by the politic of apartheid. This sensitive person could not thrive in such an environment. She was very close to Rea, I remember.

By Keith

I loved my Aunty Thay. She was always so pretty and nice and sweet and charming. She gave Valda and me a little red teapot as a wedding present, which we use to this day. Shortly before she died, she and I went for a walk together around the Zoo Lake in Jhb and then had tea in Rosebank. It was a lovely time.

5. Lichtenstein, **Edwin**

b: 24 March 1923, S. Africa
d: 2 March 2004, London, UK
m: Leonie Globus
occ: Lawyer

Figure 6.20.

Memories

By Keith

It was December 1959, the height of apartheid South Africa, and whites ruled Rhodesia. Russel and I were on a great three-week adventure, hitch-hiking around Rhodesia. First stop was Bulawayo to visit our highly-intelligent, political, Uncle Ed and Leonie. I think by that stage they had fled, or been forced, to leave South Africa because of their very liberal activities. Russel and I were somewhat taken aback when the only other guests were a black Rhodesian couple; but they were delightful and also most intelligent. This was the first time we had actually socialized and had a meal with a black couple. We felt that Edwin had done this simply to make a point: a lesson well learned.

Great-Grandchildren

Great-Grandchildren of Johanna Graudan and Julius Holzberg (n=18, 16 Biol.):
Hilda Rabinowitz (Buhai) Family (n=1)

1. Leftin, **Penny**

b: 1947, S. Africa (adopted by Henry and Hilda Leftin)

Figure 6.21.

Great-Grandchildren of Johanna Graudan and Julius Holzberg:
David Rabinowitz (Buhai) Family (n=1)

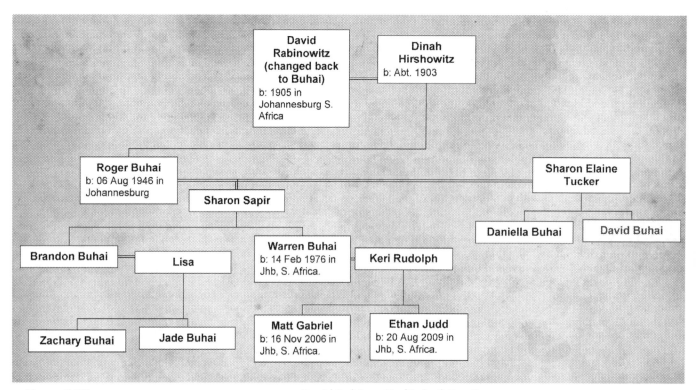

Figure 6.22.   David Rabinowitz (Buhai) Family

1. Buhai, **Roger**

b: 6 Aug. 1946, Johannesburg, S. Africa (adopted by David and Dinah Buhai)
m: Sharon Sapir (divorced)
m: Sharon Elaine Tucker
occ: Buyer for Rich's Food
rec: Snooker, pool, billiards, card games, reading currently: Johannesburg

Figure 6.23.

Great-Grandchildren of Johanna Graudan and Julius Holzberg:
Thelma Rabinowitz Family (n=2)

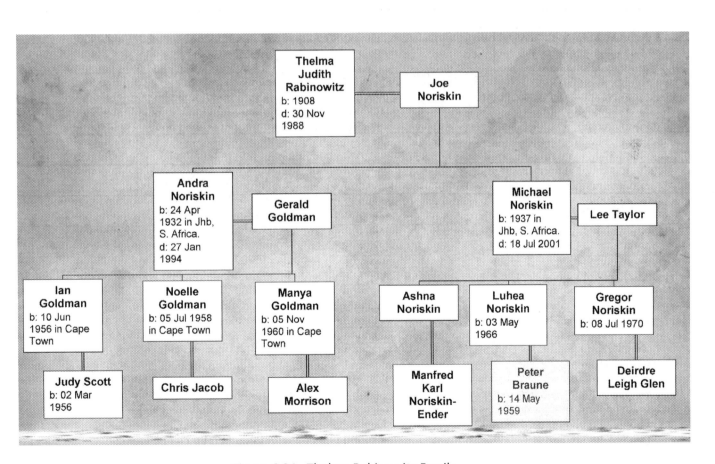

Figure 6.24. Thelma Rabinowitz Family

1. Noriskin, **Andra**

b: 24 Apr. 1932, S. Africa
d: 27 Jan. 1994
m: Gerald Goldman, 1955, London, UK
occ: Occupational therapist, librarian, psychotherapist
rec: Pottery

Figure 6.25.

Memories

By son Ian Goldman

Andra was born in 1932 of parents Thelma Rabinowitz and Joe Noriskin. She attended Parktown Girls School, and studied occupational therapy at Wits University. After graduating she went to the UK, where she met Gerald, the brother of her schoolfriend Audrey Goldman (now Coleman). Gerald and Andra married in London in 1955 and then returned to South Africa where Ian was born in 1956. They lived in Cape Town from 1956–60. Noelle was born in 1958 and Manya in 1960. Gerald was jailed for his political activities in 1960 in the First Emergency. After that, they moved to Durban, where Gerald lectured at the Architecture Department. Andra worked as a librarian at the University. She also trained as a potter.

In 1965 after Gerald's career was damaged as a PhD scholarship was refused because of his political background, they moved to the UK. Andra worked as an occupational therapist in the UK and also taught pottery. She later worked for the National Association for Mental Health and finally qualified as a psychotherapist, which she loved. Andra was a very passionate person, with a huge heart, and she was much loved by many. She died in 1994 after her heart valve failed on her way to a pottery class.

2. Noriskin, **Michael**

b: 26 Oct. 1937, Johannesburg, S. Africa
d: 18 July 2001
m: Lee Taylor, 22 Sept 1962

Figure 6.26.

Great-Grandchildren of Johanna Graudan and Julius Holzberg:
Sheila Rabinowitz Family (n=4)

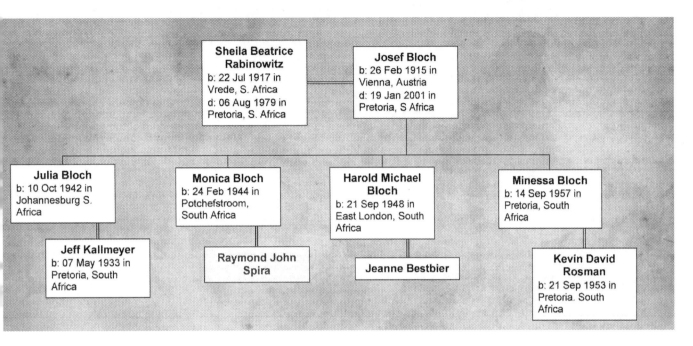

Figure 6.27. Sheila Rabinowitz Family

1. Bloch, **Julia**

b: 10 Oct. 1942, Johannesburg, S. Africa
m: Jeff Kallmeyer, 28 Dec 1966, Pretoria
occ: Retired teacher
rec: Music, theatre, gym, needlepoint
currently: Toronto, Canada

Figure 6.28.

Personal Story

We moved here, to Toronto, two and half years ago. Stan and Ing have been living here for the past seventeen years and we wanted to be with them and our three beloved grandchildren. The boys are both in Phoenix, Arizona, with their families. We spend the whole, or nearly the whole, winter there with them. Ian has a beautiful cottage in his garden where we stay. Arizona is absolutely beautiful in winter and there are gorgeous places to visit around there; e.g., Sedona, Flagstaff, the Grand Canyon, etc. So we consider ourselves unbelievably lucky.

We really love Toronto as we are very into music and theater and, of course, there is so much available to do and see here. Besides which it is such a beautiful city.

Jeff has totally retired from medicine but keeps very busy playing tennis, working in our little garden, walking the dogs, etc. I am also not teaching anymore, but I keep busy with the children and grandchildren, working out in the gym, needlepoint, etc.

This year is very busy with a bar mitzvah, a new baby, and going to Israel at the end of the year, and then on to S.A. for a family wedding.

2. Bloch, **Monica**

b: 24 Feb. 1944, Potchefstroom, S. Africa
m: Raymond John Spira, 5 July 1967, Pretoria
occ: Mathematics teacher
currently: Johannesburg

Figure 6.29.

3. Bloch, **Harold Michael**

b: 21 Sept. 1948, East London, S. Africa
m: Jeanne Constance Bestbier, 2 Sept. 1979, Pretoria
occ: Gastroenterologist/physician, part-time protea farmer
rec: Wildlife and nature photography, golf, high-altitude hiking, scuba diving, pilot [fully instrument-rated 2,800 hours], mountain and road cycling, horse riding
currently: Stonebridge Farm, Stellenbosch, S. Africa

Figure 6.30.

Curriculum Vitae

Education: Matriculated Kearsney College Natal
                  MB. Ch, B [cum Laude] Pretoria, FCP [South Africa] 1978, MRCP [UK] 1980, FRCP [UK] 1993

Positions held: Chief Gastroenterology, Johannesburg General Hospital 1981–1985
                  Part-time Chief Gastroenterology, Johannesburg Hospital 1985- 1987
                  Private Practice, Johannesburg 1985–1996
                  Private Practice, Somerset West 1996–Present
                  Part-time consultant, Groote Schuur Hospital 1996–2008

4. Bloch, **Minessa**

b: 14 Sept. 1957, Pretoria, S. Africa
m: Kevin David Rosman, 26 Nov. 1978, Pretoria
currently: Johannesburg

Figure 6.31.

Great-Grandchildren of Johanna Graudan and Julius Holzberg:
Josse Kaye (Josiah Kaplan) Family (n=2)

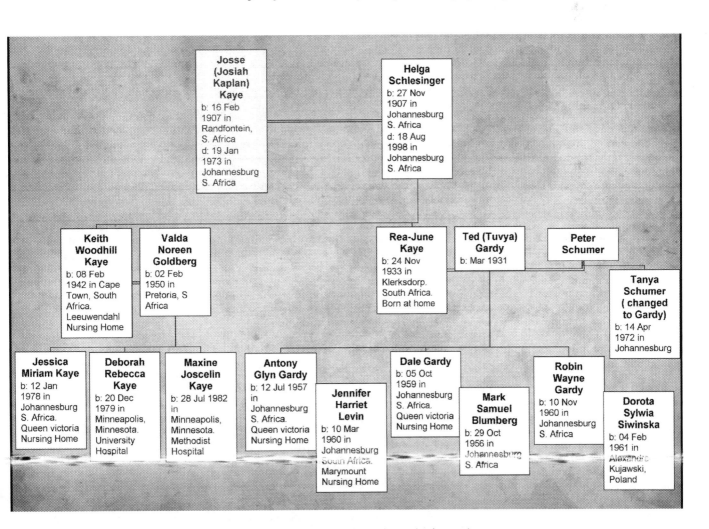

Figure 6.32. Josse Kaye (Josiah Kaplan) Family

1. Kaye, **Rea-June**

b: 24 November 1933, Klerksdorp, S. Africa
m: Ted Gardy, 16 October 1955 (divorced)
m: Peter Schumer
occ: Dress designer
rec: Exercise, friends, studying French
currently: Plettenberg Bay, S. Africa

Figure 6.33.

Personal Story

Written April 2004; addressed to her brother Keith

Boykie, let's hope this works! Managed to get up the biography email I sent you, intending to delete and add the bits you wanted. But no way could I get the bloody cursor to appear—no way!!! So I'll write the bits you asked for and you'll have to put them where you think they should go. I'm so sorry! Another inexplicable phenomenon. Wherever I put an apostrophe in my email to you, when I printed out your reply, they ALL show up as ? marks. Oh well, all this modern technology is way over my little head. I'll try and help you edit. . . .

I was born at home in Klerksdorp, three days before Mom's birthday. I was her birthday present. Yes, I was born in that little house in Klerksdorp, but have no idea why. Sadly, it never occurred to me to ask. I only know Mom had been invited out to tea that morning, but I arrived instead. [Keith was born eight days before Dad's birthday. He was Dad's best present ever.]

At fifteen months, left for England, where we stayed until I was seven years old. Our first stay was in a little boarding house, (I think in Brixton, I'm almost positive) belonging to a dear couple Mr. and Mrs. Corey, who apparently doted on me, and whom I called Granny and Grampa. It was there whilst looking at birds kept in an aviary, that I told my first lie (aged two). I believe I had an accident in my panties. When Mom saw the puddle on the ground and berated me, I said "Dunie didn't do it—birdie did it!"

An aside . . . Much to my disgust, Mom always called me June, instead of Rea, because she had a slight speech impediment and rolled her Rs and didn't want me to start doing the same. This continued till my teens, when I made an all-out effort to be called by my preferred name. If I was called June/Junie or Junikins, I just refused to answer!

We then moved to a flat in Maida Vale, where we stayed until war broke out; then we moved to Ashtead in Surrey to a semi-detached house. It was here that Dad bought me my first very own dog, a wire-haired terrier named Chippy, which I adored. I would dress him in doll's clothes (I never, ever liked dolls, only teddy bears and cuddlies!), put him in a doll's pram, and take the poor thing for a walk!

It was at this time we were told at school that if there was an air-raid siren, either going to school or on the way home from it, we were to run to whichever was the closest. I clearly remember, just having left the school grounds, when there was a siren and I made the decision to run all the way home, no matter what the consequences. It was then, too, that we were taught how to put on our gas masks, which all the children carried over their shoulders. I was six.

It was during this time, too, that Dad had an air-raid shelter built at the bottom of our little garden. It was supposed to be strong enough to withstand any bombing, except a direct hit. It was built mainly for my protection. This was a great sacrifice by both Mom and Dad, as Dad was still a student studying medicine in London and they had very little money. This shelter was the only thing that really belonged to them in the seven years we lived in England.

One quite sweet story . . . The bell to our house didn't work, so Mom pinned a note to the door saying, "Please knock, don't ring." That night whilst we were safely asleep in our shelter, a bomb fell on the house across the road. The blast was so strong it blew in our front door. In the morning we all rushed out to see exactly what had happened, when I saw the note on the door, I said to Mom, "Look Mommy, the Germans have left us a note!"

We returned to SA during World War II, on an old passenger ship—it's last voyage. The trip from Southampton to Cape Town took six weeks, as we were chased off course by enemy submarines (U-boats) as far as Greenland.

We lived in the Cape, where Keith was born in 1942, spending periodic holidays with Gran and Grampa in Johannesburg, until we moved there permanently in 1945. I attended thirteen schools, as we moved around, including a two-year stay at Potch Girls High, (which I hated) until I was "asked to leave." I matriculated at Barnato Park, where I turned seventeen during my final exams.

My first love was the theater, but Dad wouldn't hear of my traveling away from Joh'burg. He said I was too temperamental (90 percent temper and 10 percent mental) and was not happy to let me out of his sight. I wasn't even allowed to go to Europe with a friend. With Mom as chaperone—*yea sure*. I opted out of that one.

Instead, I became a dress designer. I met and married Ted on Oct. 16, 1955; I had my first three children, Antony (born July 12, 1957), Dale (born Oct. 5, 1959), and Robin (born Nov. 10, 1960). We lived in boring suburbia, until our divorce in 1970. Made the grave error of marrying Peter Schumer. After only fifteen months of a turbulent marriage, which both Mom and Dad were dead against, this too ended in divorce. But beforehand, little Tanya was born, two to three months premature. When she was seven months old, I met Bernard with whom I lived for twenty-one years. These were the best and most amazing years of my life. Being eleven-and-a-half-years younger than me, it was inevitable as I grew older he would eventually leave, which he did in 1993. But he has been remarkable, still taking care of Tanya and me financially, something he is not legally bound to do. He is an honorable man. I have been very lucky.

And now ten years later, as I have reached my seventh decade, I am about to embark on a totally new way of life. The previous eight years with Tanya were wonderful, in spite of her having to undergo numerous operations and suffer many setbacks. Then came the catastrophic seventeenth operation, with the ensuing fracture three weeks later, which led to a two-year downhill, mental and emotional spiral. After the inevitable eighteenth op, to correct the non-union, which seems to be a success, it appears she is regaining her old self. Now with the unbelievable help from Keith and Valda, we will be going to live in Plettenberg Bay. This will be the fifth and final phase of my life. Let me explain . . . I have always said I have experienced five totally different lives, within one lifetime.

  1) My early childhood in England
  2) My growing up years in S.A., including my marriage, children, etc.
  3) My life with Bernard, including holidays abroad, travel, togetherness—such a good life. I always said that I was enjoying for two decades what most people don't experience in a lifetime.
  4) My life alone with Tanya. The ten years devoting myself to trying to assure her future.

This has not been an easy life.

And now, the fifth and final phase in Plettenberg Bay. Let's hold thumbs for this one!!!
Crikes, I did it! But I got the message repeated about four times and I've spent ages getting rid of the extra three!!! Such an a-h!

Is this the sort of thing you're looking for? If it's okay, I'll do one for Tanya.
Keithie, it was shortly after my birth that Daddy wrote that beautiful tribute to his mother. I have got it somewhere and as soon as I get settled and unpacked I'm sure I'll find it. You must leave space for this, or else don't do anything final till you've included it.

I love you, my boy,
Re

2. Kaye, **Keith Woodhill**

b: 8 Feb 1942, Cape Town, S. Africa
m: Valda Noreen Goldberg, 10 October 1973, Pretoria, S. Africa
occ: Urologist, urology professor (U. Western Australia), medical software content developer
rec: Sports: water skiing, snow skiing, biking, running, kayaking; also studying genealogy, genetic genealogy, and Hebrew, archaeology (esp biblical); making home movies; cars; traveling
currently: Minnneapolis, Minnesota, USA

Figure 6.34.

Personal Story

We lived in Cape Town until I was three, and then moved to Johannesburg. The first six years of school were at Parkview, and my high school was Parktown Boys High. My main interests during school were sports and Boy Scouts. One of the highlights was at age fifteen when I became a Queen's Scout and represented South Africa at the Jubilee Jamboree (fiftieth anniversary of Scouting and one hundredth anniversary of Baden-Powell's birth) in Great Britain. An added bonus was missing three and a half months of school as we traveled by ship!

Following that, I went to Medical School at the University of Witwatersrand, where I became interested in paleoanthropology; thus, I studied two extra years for a BSc (Hons), before graduating as a Doctor of Medicine. At University I was Chairman of the Rag Committee, a boisterous fund-raising and spirit-raising (in all senses of the word) organization. In the clinical years, I was class president. As a student I would work as a waiter, save money, and then on the long summer holidays I would hitch-hike around Rhodesia and Europe to explore caves (getting Cave's Disease in the process) and go on kayak expeditions down the Orange, Tugela, and other S. African rivers.

Then I spent seven years specializing in general surgery under the superb, but formidable, Professor DJ du Plessis, and I spent a further four years in Urologic Surgery getting degrees FCS (SA) General Surgery, FCS(SA) Urology, FRCS (Edin). During this time it was wonderful having my father as the Professor of Radiology.

Before getting into the intensive part of general surgery training I took off a year to travel. I worked in a Circus in Switzerland (Zirkus Stey) for a month; as a roustabout—not a clown! Then I spent another month kayaking around Holland with a Dutch girlfriend, joined the "First British Grand Canyon Canoe Expedition" to kayak down the Colorado River, and competed in the Liffey Descent—a kayak race through Dublin, Ireland.

The best thing that ever happened to me was marrying Valda Goldberg. At the time she had just obtained her medical degree. We went to Victoria Falls and Chobe Game Reserve, staying in a room with our own private swimming pool and adjacent to the room that Elizabeth Taylor and Richard Burton had occupied a few weeks earlier on for their honeymoon (second, I believe).

Before specializing in Urology, Valda and I dropped out for four months, traveling to Mauritius, Seychelles, Hong Kong, and Papua New Guinea, where we spent six weeks exploring in dugout canoes, hiking, camping, and collecting oceanic art.

Having specialized in Urology in South Africa, I was invited to join the Urology Department at the University of Minnesota. Ostensively we were planning to stay in the US for three years, however it eventuated that we never did return to RSA to live permanently. Our eldest daughter Jessica was born in South Africa nineteen months before coming to the States. Deborah and Maxine were both born in Minneapolis. In Minnesota, I became interested in outpatient surgery and published the first textbook in the field called "Outpatient Urologic Surgery." I also developed a catheter that has come to be called the "Kaye Nephrostomy Tamponade Catheter," produced by Cook Urology.

In the early 1990s I was invited to introduce Prostate Ultrasound to Australia. This resulted a few years later in my being appointed as the first Professor of Urology in Australia at the University of Western Australia in Perth. This was a difficult time. For six years the Kaye Family commuted between Minneapolis, Minnesota, and Perth, Australia. (About as far apart as one can get on this planet!) The girls each spent six months at school with me in Australia. Eventually the situation became untenable and despite my best efforts to lure Valda and the girls, what with a magnificent cliffside house in a very special Swan Riverside pocket of Perth, called "The Coombe," I retired my position and returned to Minneapolis. During my time in Australia my main interest was prostate cancer and the anatomy and function of the small muscle that maintains urinary continence. I also introduced and taught courses on brachytherapy, a technique of treating prostate cancer.

Returning to the US, I did not have the heart to join another department or set up a private practice. I was extremely fortunate to be invited to develop the urologic content for a medical software company, now called ProVation Medical. Some ten years later (in 2010), this is where I very happily remain working part-time.

Other than work, in summer I enjoy water-skiing and biking, in winter I enjoy snow-skiing, studying genealogy (genetic genealogy) and trying to learn Hebrew. I travel to Belize several times a year to do voluntary urology work at the Western Regiona Hospital in Belmopan, which I thoroughly enjoy, and we have also started a teak plantation. One recent project, which gave me tremendous satisfaction, was helping the current small Jewish population of Panevezys, Lithuania, to build a memorial to the old Jewish Cemetery in Panevezys, which had been totally destroyed by the Lithuanian Soviets in 1966.

I am incredibly lucky and fortunate to have had, and continue to have, an amazing life. I had the most loving and supportive parents and close friend as an adored sister. I married the best girl, have three incredible daughters, and maybe as a partial completion of my life's circle, our middle daughter Deborah, qualified as a doctor and is going into the field of urology. She has started training at the institution that has been rated as the top in the US for the past nineteen years—Johns Hopkins in Baltimore. Of the three accepted for training, Deborah was the only one who came from outside (from an undergraduate school other than Hopkins).

I have been, and am, truly blessed!

Great-Grandchildren of Johanna Graudan and Julius Holzberg:
Bernard Lichtenstein (Leyton) Family (n=2)

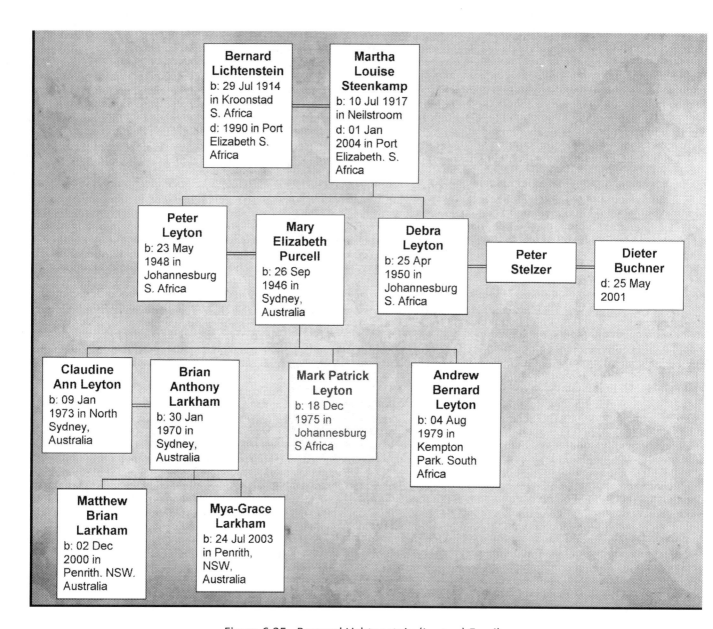

Figure 6.35. Bernard Lichtenstein (Leyton) Family

1.Leyton, **Peter**

b: 23 May 1948, Johannesburg, S. Africa
m: Mary Elizabeth Purcell, Australia
occ: Graphic Repro (Printing)
rec: Working on and riding motor bikes, reading, walking, chess, digital photography, aircraft, canoeing, golfing, working on my Triumph Bonneville currently: Tea Gardens, NSW, Australia

Figure 6.36.

2. Leyton, **Debra Rebecca**

b: 25 April 1950, Johannesburg, S. Africa
m: Peter Stelzer (divorced)
m: Dieter Buechner
occ: Teacher
rec: Yoga, hiking, and dancing. Caring for animals, especially cats. Reading, being with friends.
currently: Zurich, Switzerland

Figure 6.37.

Personal Story

Schooling: Jeppe Prep and matriculated Jeppe Girls High; Greenoaks Finishing School.

Attended ballet from three to seventeen years, then did Latin American dancing and became S.A. Champion in 1968.

Worked at Johannesburg Stock Exchange in experiment as woman trader (playing on big mouth) and transferred to London for one year. Returned and shortly afterwards met first husband, Peter Stelzer, and went to live in Switzerland. Married from 1976 to 1983.

Divorced. Remarried, Dieter Buechner, 1985. Widowed 2001. No children. Earn daily bread teaching English.

Great-Grandchildren of Johanna Graudan and Julius Holzberg:
Thalia Lichtenstein Family (n=4)

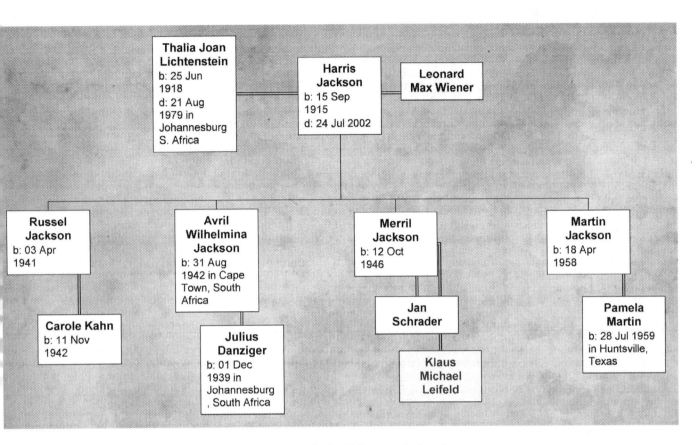

Figure 6.38. Thalia Lichtenstein Family

1. Jackson, **Russel**

b: 3 April 1941, S. Africa
m: Carole Kahn
occ: Radiologist
rec: Keeping fit
currently: Boston, Massachusets, USA

Figure 6.39.

Personal Story

Dr. Jackson grew up in Johannesburg. He received his medical degree from the University of Pretoria in 1966, South Africa, and specialized in radiology at Groote Schuur Hospital in Cape Town in 1971. He immigrated to the USA and did a Fellowship in Radiology at the University Hospital in Boston. He currently practices at South Shore Hospital, S. Weymouth, Massachusetts, specializing in diagnostic radiology.

2. Jackson, **Avril Wilhelmina**

b: 31 Aug 1942, Cape Town, S. Africa
m: Julius Danziger
occ: Retired School Teacher
currently: Houston, Texas, USA

Figure 6.40.

3. Jackson, **Merril**

b: 12 Oct. 1946, S. Africa
m: Jan. Schrader (divorced)
m: Klaus Michael Leifeld
occ: Anesthesiologist
currently: Germany

Figure 6.41.

Personal Story

I still do some anaesthesia but mainly pain therapy. I have private practice rooms in Witten, not far from home. I sing in a choir and take lessons with my darling professor. Will probably slow down working pace at the end of next year, when I'll be sixty-five.

4. Jackson, **Martin**

b: 18 Apr. 1958, S. Africa
m: Pamela Martin
occ: Podiatrist
currently: Mesquite, Texas, USA

Figure 6.42.

Great-Grandchildren of Johanna Graudan and Julius Holzberg:
Edwin Lichtenstein Family (n=2)

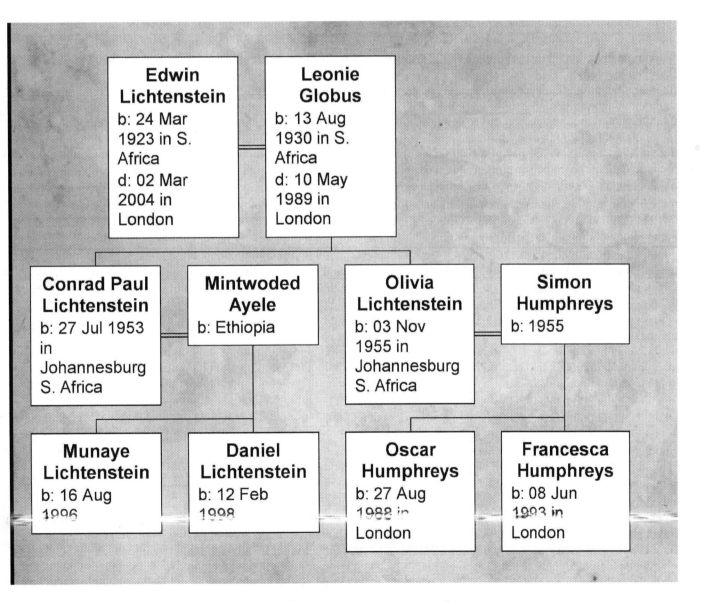

Figure 6.43. Edwin Lichtenstein Family

1. Lichtenstein, **Conrad Paul**

b: 27 July 1953, Johannesburg, S. Africa
m: Mintwoded Ayele 3 Sept. 1995, Washington DC
occ: Molecular Biologist
currently: London, UK

Figure 6.44.

Biography

Professor Conrad Lichtenstein, PhD, is Vice President for Research and Development of Population Genetics Technologies [PGT], Ltd., a biotech startup company based in the Babraham Research Campus, Cambridge. PGT is developing novel technology, conceived by Nobel laureate Professor Sydney Brenner, to sample large populations to identify the genetic variation responsible for human disease and drug response.

Conrad has over thirty years of research experience working in the field of molecular biology and biotechnology with over eighty publications. He obtained his PhD in molecular biology from Cambridge University, working under Nobel laureate Sydney Brenner at the MRC Laboratory of Molecular Biology. After a post-doctoral fellowship at the University of Washington in Seattle, he returned in 1983 to a faculty position at Imperial College, University of London. He then spent a sabbatical year at the National Cancer Institute, Frederick, Maryland, USA, returning to London as Chair of Molecular Biology at Queen Mary, University of London from 1996–2005. He is a board director of Westgate Hall, plc.—a VC fund established in January 2002 to make primarily seed investments in biotechnology and information technology.

At the University of London, his research group was the first to use RNA silencing to engineer resistance to virus infection in genetically-modified plants; this led to an invitation from scientists in Pakistan to collaborate, with public-sector funding, to produce GM cotton plants with resistance to a serious endemic viral pathogen that reduces yields of this important cash crop by 30 percent.

He also discovered that the very genes his laboratory were inserting into plants had jumped in 25 million years earlier, thus showing that genetic modification can occur in nature. This discovery led to his engagement in the GM debate and he is committed to the public understanding of science and has written on genetic modification issues and other topics for the broadsheet press. He is a panel member of Cropgen, a consumer and media information initiative. CropGen's mission is to make the case for GM crops by helping to achieve a greater measure of realism and a better balance in the UK public debate about crop biotechnology. And in this capacity he has given radio, TV, and newspaper interviews, and he has participated in public debates as well as given guest lectures on genetics to secondary schools.

Academic Record

Vice President for Research and Development, January 2005–present, Population Genetics Technologies, Ltd., Babraham Research Campus, Babraham, Cambridgeshire, CB22 3AT.

Visiting Professor of Molecular Biology, January 2006–Present, School of Biological and Chemical Sciences, Queen Mary, University of London.

Professor of Molecular Biology, January 1996–December 2005, School of Biological Sciences, Queen Mary, University of London.

January 2005–December 2005, one-year unpaid leave of absence.

Sabbatical Visitor, October 1994–October 1995. Laboratory of Eukaryotic Gene Expression, ABL-Basic Research Program, NCI-Frederick Cancer Research & Development Center, Frederick, Maryland, USA. Project: Analysis of host factors regulating transposition of the LTR-retro-transposon, Ty1, in the budding yeast S. cerevisiae.

Lecturer in Genetic Engineering, June 1983 to December 1995, Centre for Biotechnology, Department of Biochemistry, Imperial College of Science Technology & Medicine, University of London, UK.

Postdoctoral research fellow, March 1981 to May 1983. Department of Microbiology & Immunology, University of Washington, Seattle, Washington, USA. Project: Molecular analysis of the T-DNA of Agrobacterium tumefaciens.

MRC research fellow, October 1979 to February 1981. MRC Laboratory of Molecular Biology, Cambridge, England.

MRC research student, October 1976 to September 1979, MRC Laboratory of Molecular Biology, Cambridge, England; plus King's College, University of Cambridge, PhD, December 1980. PhD thesis title: "The Unique Insertion Site of Transposon Tn7 in the Escherichia Coli Chromosome." PhD supervisor: Dr. Sydney Brenner, FRS, Nobel Laureate 2002.

British Council/CONACYT exchange research student February 1976 to September 1976. Departaménto de Biología Molecular, Centro des Investigacíones y Estudios Avanzados del Instituto Politecnico Nacional, Mexico City, Mexico. Project: Development of methods for the detection of heat-stable enterotoxins of pathogenic strains of Escherichia coli.

Laboratory technician, September 1975 to January 1976, Immunology Group, Department of Anatomy, University College, University of London, London. Project: Characterisation of tumour-specific antigens of a human neuroblastoma.

Laboratory technician June to August 1975, Unit of Nitrogen Fixation, University of Sussex,

Brighton, Sussex, UK. Project: Characterization of mutations in the nitrogenous gene on

Klebsiella pneumonia.

Undergraduate education 1972–1975. School of Biological Sciences, University of Sussex.

Bsc (Hon.) degree in biology, 1975, First in Class.

Fellowships

April 1982–May 1983 SERC-NATO two-year postdoctoral traveling fellowship [resigned May 1983 to take up appointment at Imperial College].

February 1981, elected a Research Fellow of Jesus College, University of Cambridge [resigned October 1983 to take up appointment at Imperial College].

April 2000, elected a Fellow of the Royal Society of Arts.

December 2000, elected a Member of the Royal Institution.

Languages

Reasonably fluent in Spanish, with a basic knowledge of French and German.

2. Lichtenstein, **Olivia**

b: 3 Nov. 1955, Johannesburg, S. Africa
m: Simon Humphreys
occ: Writer, Film Director
currently: London, UK

Figure 6.45.

Books Published

Chloe Zhivago's Recipe for Marriage and Mischief
Things Your Mother Never Told You

* * *

Great-Great-Grandchildren

Great-Great-Grandchildren of Johanna Graudan and Julius Holzberg (n=43; 39 Biol.):
Roger Buhai Family (n=4)

1. Buhai, **Brandon**

Figure 6.46.

2. Buhai, **Warren**

> b: 14 Feb. 1976, Johannesburg, S. Africa
> m: Keri Rudolph
> occ: Finance
> rec: Soccer, rugby, cricket, non-fiction books, movies, TV series, family
> currently: Johannesburg

Figure 6.47.

Personal Story

I was born in Jhb and apart from living in the US (Boca Raton, Florida) from September '07 to January '09, I've lived in Jhb all my life. I am currently a portfolio manager at STANLIB (part of the Standard Bank group), where I joined in 2005 (and rejoined after returning from the US, where I was the Managing Director of Investments at a private wealth-management firm called Levitt Capital Management, LLP). Prior to moving into asset management, I spent five years in Corporate Finance at Standard Bank and prior to that I spent six years at Ernst & Young. I am a qualified CA(SA) and CFA charterholder (I did my BCompt and BCompt Honors degrees part time through the University of South Africa).

Interests: Soccer (play, watch, talk, eat, sleep, and drink it), rugby, cricket, non-fiction reading, movies, TV series addict (thrillers such as Dexter; and British comedy) and last and most importantly, family time.

3. Buhai, **Daniella**

b: 5 July 1985, Johannesburg, S. Africa
occ: Gemologist
rec: Reading, going to the gym, shopping
currently: Johannesburg

Figure 6.48.

4. Buhai, **David**

b: 27 May 1976, Johannesburg, S. Africa
occ: Currently professional golf caddy on European Ladies Tour
rec: Golf, football, cricket, soccer

Figure 6.49.

Great-Great-Grandchildren of Johanna Graudan and Julius Holzberg:
Andra Noriskin Family (n=3)

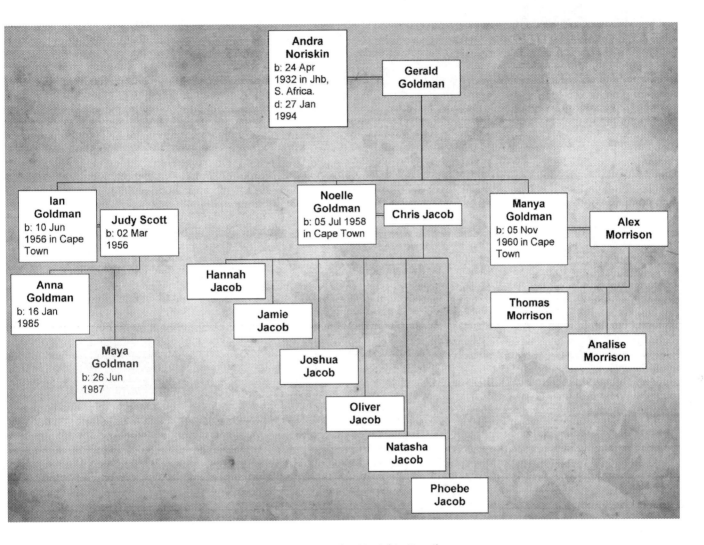

Figure 6.50. Andra Noriskin Family

1. Goldman, Ian (Siphiwe)

b: 10 June 1956, Cape Town, S. Africa
m: Judy Scott
occ: PhD in Public and Development Management; worked in rural development, community-driven development, and currently on project with Presidency in S. Africa

Figure 6.51.

2. Goldman, **Noelle**

b: 5 July 1958 , S. Africa
m: Chris Jacob
occ: Cultural Consultant

Figure 6.52.

3. Goldman, **Manya**

b: 5 Nov. 1960, S. Africa
m: Alex Morrison

Figure 6.53.

Great-Great-Grandchildren of Johanna Graudan and Julius Holzberg:
Michael Noriskin Family (n = 3)

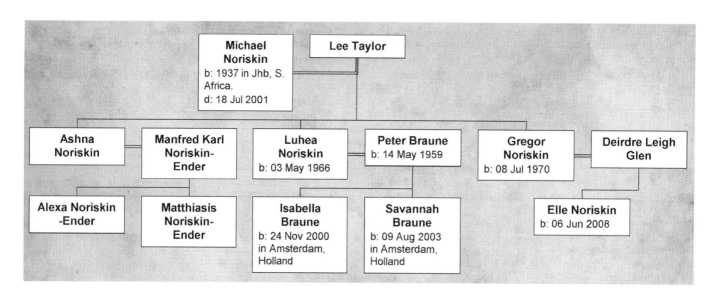

Figure 6.54. Michael Noriskin Family

1. Noriskin, **Ashna**

b: 18 Nov. 1967, Jhb, S. Africa
m: Manfred Karl Ender

Figure 6.55.

2. Noriskin, **Luhea**

b: 3 May 1966
m: Peter Rudolph Braune, 25 April 1991, Amsterdam, Holland
currently: Amsterdam, Holland

3. Noriskin, **Gregor**

b: 8 July 1970
occ: Software architect
currently: Vancouver, Canada

Figure 6.56.

Personal Story

Gregor Noriskin was born on July 8, 1970, in Cape Town, South Africa. His family moved to Johannesburg in 1971. He attended Glenhazel Primary School, and then Highlands North Boys High School, where he matriculated in 1988. In 1989 he began studying Civil Engineering at the University of the Witwatersrand (Wits), but did not finish.

In 1990 Gregor did his national service at 1 Parachute Battalion in Tempe, Bloemfontein. He went back to

Wits in 1991 to study Computer Science and Archeology. After a year and a half, Gregor finally resigned himself to the fact that he was not cut out for academia, and went traveling in Europe. He returned to South Africa in 1993 and worked for a number of small companies, assembling computer hardware and writing software. In 1994 Gregor joined Systems Programming Limited (SPL) as a software developer. SPL gave him the opportunity to travel to the US to research the then-emerging Internet, and returned to South Africa as one of the first Internet Development Consultants in the country. In 1996 he joined The Internet Solution (IS), which was South Africa's largest Internet Service Provider at the time, as Senior Software Architect. He stayed with IS until 1998, and then joined Microsoft South Africa as a Software Development Consultant. Though he was based in South Africa, Gregor spent most of the two years with Microsoft South Africa working on large-scale e-commerce projects in Sweden, Italy, the USA, and Australia (and spent almost no time in South Africa).

In 2000, Gregor moved to Microsoft's headquarters in the USA, located in Redmond, Washington. He spent nearly a decade with Microsoft, working in various technical roles. The high point of his career with Microsoft was working as the Technical Assistant to the CTO.

While he was at Microsoft, Gregor met Deirdre Glen, who was then studying International Relations at the University of British Columbia in Vancouver, Canada. They dated for a couple of years and then were married on the beach in Vancouver on February 10, 2006. Deirdre and Gregor moved to New York shortly after getting married, and lived in Williamsburg, where they stayed until the end of 2007. Gregor and Deirdre decided that they wanted to start a family and could not think of a better place to do that than Vancouver. Gregor also took this as an opportunity to try his hand at video game development and joined Electronic Arts Canada. On June 6, 2008 Deirdre gave birth to their daughter Elle.

In 2009, Gregor lost his job at EA and spent eight months playing with his daughter and weathering the worst job market since the Great Depression. In December of 2009, Gregor joined Colligo Networks Incorporated, where he still works as Product Architect. Gregor and Deirdre are expecting their second child, a son, in September. Gregor is an avid reader of science fiction, philosophy, physics, neurology, cooking, and recently children's books.

Great-Great-Grandchildren of Johanna Graudan and Julius Holzberg: Julia Bloch Family (n=3)

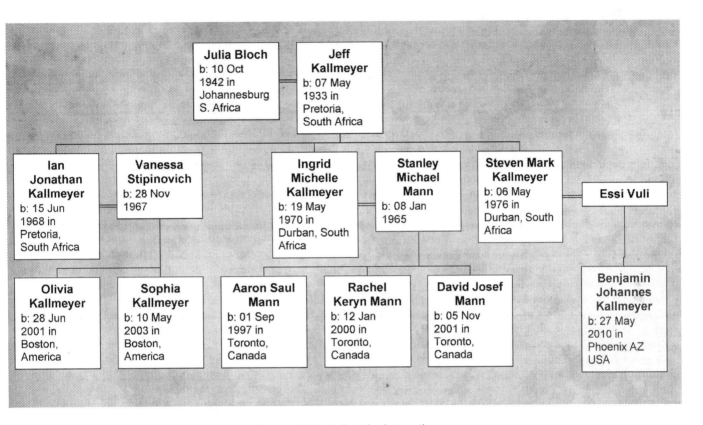

Figure 6.57. Julia Bloch Family

1. Kallmeyer, **Ian Jonathan**

b: 15 June 1968, Pretoria, S.Africa
occ: Anaesthesiologist
m: Vanessa Stipinovich, 24 January 1999, Cape Town
currently: Phoeniz, Arizona, USA

Figure 6.58.

2. Kallmeyer, **Ingrid Michelle**

b: 19 May 1970, Durban, S. Africa
m: Stanley Michael Mann, 1 Aug. 1994, Durban
currently: Toronto, Canada

Figure 6.59.

3. Kallmeyer, **Steven Mark**

b: 6 May 1976, Durban. S. Africa
occ: : Anaesthesiologist
m: Essi Vuli, 30 Aug. 2008, Boston
currently: Phoeniz, Arizona, USA

Figure 6.60.

Great-Great-Grandchildren of Johanna Graudan and Julius Holzberg: Monica Bloch Family (n=4)

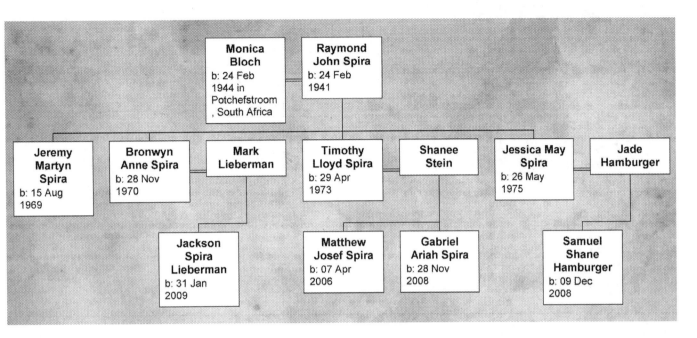

Figure 6.61. Monica Bloch Family

1. Spira, **Jeremy Martyn**

> b: 15 Aug. 1969, Johannesburg, S.Africa
> occ: Investment consultant
> m: Allison Getz, 5 Jan. 2011
> currently: London, UK

Figure 6.62.

Personal Story

Went to Highlands North Boys' High School, Johannesburg from 1983–81 and then University of Cape Town from 1988–92, obtaining B.A.Sc. Worked at PSI Actuarial Solutions in Cape Town as a partner from 2001–2003; Then moved to Johannesburg to work as a senior consultant at Alexander Forbes. From 2007 to present, I have been working as an associate at Mercer, in London.

2. Spira, **Bronwyn Anne**

b: 28 Nov. 1970
m: Mark Lieberman, 24 Nov. 2007

Figure 6.63.

3. Spira, **Timothy Lloyd**

b: 29 Apr. 1973
m: Shanee Stein, 13 Sept. 1998

Figure 6.64.

4. Spira, **Jessica May**

b: 26 May 1975
m: Jade Hamburger, 27 Feb. 2005

Figure 6.65.

Great-Great-Grandchildren of Johanna Graudan and Julius Holzberg:
Minessa Bloch Family (n=2)

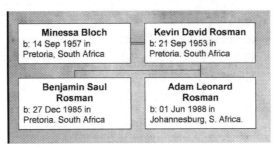

Figure 6.66. Minessa Bloch Family

1. Rosman, **Benjamin Saul**

> b: 27 Dec. 1985, Pretoria, S. Africa
> occ: PhD student, Edinburgh University
> currently: Edinburgh, Scotland

Figure 6.67.

Personal Story

By his mother Minessa

Benjamin is nearly twenty-four and is at Edinburgh University where he has just completed his Masters in Artificial Intelligence, having done a BSc in Computer Science at Wits, and then a double Honors in Computer Science and Applied Maths. He has been accepted to do his PhD in Artificial Intelligence at Edinburgh. He graduated with his masters's degree on our anniversary.

2. Rosman, **Adam Leonard**

> b: 1 June 1988, Johannesburg, S. Africa
> occ: Aeronautical engineering student, U. Witwatersrand
> currently: Johannesburg, S. Africa

Figure 6.68.

Personal Story

By his mother Minessa

Our younger son Adam is going into his final year of Aeronautical Engineering at Wits. He is twenty-one.

Great-Great-Grandchildren of Johanna Graudan and Julius Holzberg:
Rea June Kaye Family (n=4)

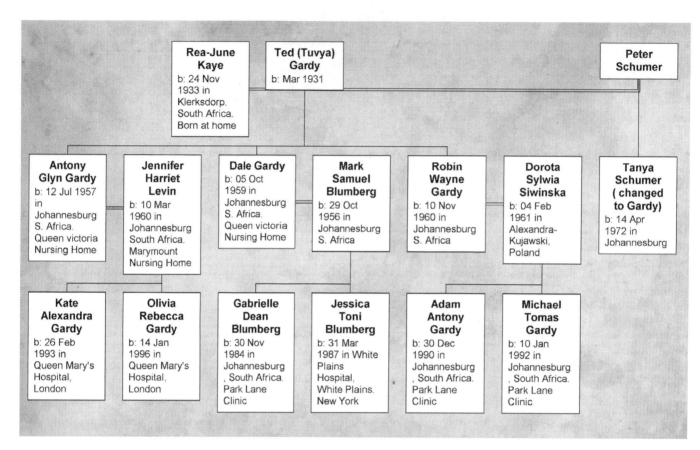

Figure 6.69. Rea June Kaye Family

1. Gardy, **Antony Glyn**

b: 12 July 1957, Johannesburg, S. Africa
m: Jennifer Harriet Levin, 19 June 1986, London, UK
occ: Dentist
rec: Hiking, cycling, running, swimming, scuba-diving, traveling, teaching tai chi chuan, motorbiking.
currently: Plettenberg Bay, S. Africa

Figure 6.70.

Personal Story

Born 1957 Queen Victoria nursing home, Johannesburg.

Schooling: Sandown Primary and High. Matriculated 1974.

Enjoyed a variety of activities, including gymnastics, rugby, cricket, athletics, swimming, tennis, Boy Cubs, Boy Scouts, camping, hiking, squash, windsurfing, cycling, etc. . . .

University of the Witwatersrand 1975–1980. Obtained BDS degree. Developed a great love of the outdoors over this period of time and spent many vacations on hiking trails. Really got to love this land and its people. Met Jen in 1978 on the beach in Plettenberg Bay.

Military service 1980–1982. Practiced as a dentist after basic training in Pretoria. Spent time at various posts, including Baragwanath Hospital and a three-month stint on "the border" (SWA/Angola) during the heat of the war. Huge learning experience. Could write an entire book just on those three months.

Worked in private dental practice in and around Johannesburg as an associate between 1982 and 1985. Moved to London in 1985, supposedly for a year or two, and stayed for eighteen. Jen joined me in London and we married on June 19, 1986. Chose date to coincide with Josse and Helga's wedding anniversary. Initially worked as an associate and in 1987 bought into a partnership in a dental practice. Enjoyed sixteen years at the practice.

New hobbies include the practice of tai chi chuan, sailing and drumming/percussion with African instruments. Time in London has been a huge period of learning and growth. Very special time that Jen and I both loved and hated. Always longed to be back at home in South Africa. At times our hearts ached for home. Finally made the decision to return.

Arrived in Plettenberg Bay in January 2003. Plett has always been Jen's and my spiritual home so it is wonderful to have realized our dream and to be living here. After an eighteenth-month sabbatical, I opened a dental practice in 2004.

UPDATE: MARCH 2010

I have been living in Plett for seven years now and I love being back HOME. My life is very full with family and work and play. My girls are fourteen and seventeen years old; they make me and Jen so proud. They excel at academics, sports, and between them music, dance, and arts.

I am interested in the surgical and prosthetic aspects of implant dentistry, both of which I thoroughly enjoy and find very stimulating. I regularly attend international implant congresses. As I practice dentistry on average three days per week, I am fortunate to have much time to nurture myself with activities that include, amongst other things, hiking, cycling, running, swimming, scuba diving, and traveling, both locally and abroad.

I continue to practice and teach tai chi chuan and enjoy spending time away with my friends on my motorbike in our beautiful surroundings, exploring the back gravel roads. This is such a stunningly beautiful country.

My marriage to Jen has been an amazing learning experience. We continue to learn so much from one another. I love her deeply and respect and admire her for the tireless work she has done on herself and for others over the years. She is an inspiration to so many people.

I am a very fortunate man to have been blessed with such an amazingly special life.

2. Gardy, **Dale**

b: 5 Oct. 1959, Johannesburg, S. Africa
m: Mark Samuel Blumberg
occ: Interior Designer
rec: Needlepointing, drawing, traveling, reading, sports spectating
currently: Westchester, New York, USA

Figure 6.71.

Personal Story

I'm an interior designer, focusing on residential interiors. This is a creative outlet discovered only in my late thirties, when I went back to school to study design, and which has landed up being both hobby and career!

I have a passion for anything that satisfies my own creativity—designing and making needlepoint rugs and pillows, designing furniture, and enhancing existing furniture pieces, drawing, etc. I love to travel to interesting parts of the world. Every place one visits adds a slightly new and fresh perspective. I'm an avid sports spectator, love to watch movies, and I love to read books set in interesting geographical, cultural, or political places/periods.

3. Gardy, **Robin Wayne**

b: 10 Nov. 1960, Johannesburg, S. Africa
m: Dorota Sylwia Siwinska
occ: Personal Banker
rec: Tennis, squash, family
currently: Rochester, New York

Figure 6.72.

Personal Story

I am a Personal Banker for JP Morgan Chase. I started out as a Stockbroker on the JHB Stock Exchange, becoming a director of Frankel Pollak, Inc. Moved to the USA with our two young sons, Adam and Michael, in 1996 to work in financial markets in New York as an emerging markets sales trader. Between the emerging markets crisis and more significantly the attack on 9/11/01, I lost my job and my ability to secure a green card. Deciding to stay in the US for the sake of our children's education and future, Dorota took a position in Canandaigua, NY on a program that allows Physicians to work in an "under-served area" for five years before becoming eligible for a Permanent Residence. The thirteen years of struggle and waiting is now behind us and our "little boys" are now in college and our greatest joy is seeing what terrific young men they have turned out to be.

Recreationally, I still enjoy playing tennis and squash, playing number 1 for my team in the first division squash league. I love spending time with my family and particularly traveling with them to new places . . . and South Africa, which never gets old.

4. Gardy, **Tanya**

b: 14 April 1972, Johannesburg, S. Africa
occ: Counseling
rec: Reading, listening to music, exercising, swimming
currently: Plettenberg Bay, S. Africa

Figure 6.73.

Personal Story

I have studied extensively since 1992. I have a great interest in psychology and counseling and am currently studying counseling skills, which I hope to develop as my life's work.

I strive to bring meaningful activities into my life each day. These include exercising, listening to music, and reading, since I have a severe type of cerebral palsy. I strive to help others and make my disability as manageable as possible!

I am really proud to be a member of the Graudan/Holzberg family.

Great-Great-Grandchildren of Johanna Graudan and Julius Holzberg:
Keith Woodhill Kaye Family (n=3)

1. Kaye, Jessica Miriam

b: 12 Jan. 1978, Johannesburg, S, Africa
occ: Actor, film student, Univ. S. California
rec: Yoga, fitness, dance, travel
currently: Los Angeles, California/New York, New York, USA

Figure 6.74.

Personal Story

I was born in Johannesburg, South Africa, and moved as a young child to the frigid winters (and humid summers) of Minneapolis, Minnesota. I attended The Blake School and enjoyed academics and athletics, music (piano as a young child), waterskiing, reading, and playing with my friends. I also discovered a deep love for the performing arts. I performed in plays and was a high-level competitive figure skater for eleven years. In 1994, I also had the opportunity to join my father Keith for a semester in Perth, Australia.

In 1996, I attended Harvard University. I created a major with the support of the university and graduated BA magna cum laude in Performance Studies. During this period, I took a year off university to work on my thesis—a dance theater piece exploring apartheid in South Africa. I also spent six months at the University of Cape Town School of Drama researching for this project.

From 2001 until the present I have been based in New York City. My first year in New York was spent training and performing as a dancer. In 2002, I entered Columbia University, and in 2005 I received an MFA in Acting. I was also the recipient of the Bob Hope Fellowship while at Columbia.

During this period (2001–present), I have had the deep pleasure of being an actress. I have toured productions in Scotland, Germany, Italy, and South Korea. I have performed regionally and in New York (including off-Broadway). I have worked in film, television, and theater, including a stint as the baddie Rebecca Lewis on the daytime soap opera "One Life to Live." Acting, and being an actress, has been and continues to be the greatest and most challenging passion of my life so far.

In recent years, I have also begun producing and directing films and live performance events. In 2007, I founded Spectrebox, a performance collaborative. With Spectrebox, I created and performed in three performance parties and choreographed and performed in a music video for the band, The Kin (www.thekin. com).

In 2008, I co-produced and starred in a short film shot in Johannesburg, South Africa, called "Gargoyle." That film was recently nominated for a 2010 SAFTA (South African Film and Television Award). This film was a transformative experience for me because I became committed to making more films; I also became committed to the idea of making art/film in South Africa again.

Since my time in South Africa, I have written, produced, and directed two short films in New York that are currently in post-production, "Night Out," a collaboration with the electronic musician Kotchy (www.kotchy. com), about a group of New York teenagers on an adventure, and "Devil's Got My Secret," a short film inspired

by the persona and music of the singer-songwriter Mieka Pauley (www.mieka.com), who is also the lead actress in the film.

In the fall of 2010, I will begin studying at the USC School of Cinematic arts in Los Angeles, California, where I will begin my enrollment in the MFA program in Film Production. I have received two scholarships to this school, which was a very personally meaningful validation to me: the Harold C. Lloyd Foundation Scholarship and the Samuel and Lorenza Gary Memorial Scholarship.

At USC and in Los Angeles I look forward to expanding my creativity, my life experiences, and my career as I learn more about acting, filmmaking, and producing and meeting new people and soaking in the sun and the new environment of the West Coast of the US!

In the future, in addition to expanding my creative passions, pursuits, and commitments, I look forward to finding an equally committed and passionate personal love as well.

2. Kaye, **Deborah Rebecca**

b: 20 Dec. 1979, Minneapolis, Minnesota, USA
occ: Physician, urology resident Johns Hopkins
rec: water skiing, running, biking, traveling, working on cars
currently: Baltimore, Mayrland, USA

Figure 6.75.

Personal Story

I was born in Minneapolis, Minnesota, and came home from the hospital dressed in a Santa Claus hat. I spent most of my time growing up in Minnesota. I absolutely loved, and continue to love, waterskiing and swimming, both of which I did competitively, and enjoyed painting. Later, I started kickboxing, which I continued for about nine years. In high school, I spent one semester studying in Israel and I spent some time at three different schools in Perth, Australia, living with my dad, waterskiing, and generally enjoying Perth.

After high school, I attended Washington University in St. Louis, where I completed my pre-medicine requirements, majored in economics, and minored in ballet. In St. Louis, I also attended paramedic school at night and worked with the St. Louis Fire Department on the ambulance. I came to k know the city well and thoroughly enjoyed my time in St. Louis, which was interspersed with random road trips. Although I thought I wanted to do medicine all of my life, I realized that the social situations I witnessed while working on the ambulance affected me greatly. So I decided to give up my thoughts of medicine, and work in public policy, trying to help people through economic and policy changes. I was fortunate to get a job at The Urban Institute in Washington DC, where I was a quantitative analyst in the Metropolitan Housing and Community Development policy center. I enjoyed my work and DC thoroughly. For a semester, I also attended culinary school and was able to drive an hour each way before work on some days to go waterskiing, which was fantastic! During this time, I continued to volunteer on the ambulance, and found that I missed dealing with patients on a daily basis. I, therefore, decided to apply for medical school and attended the Medical College of Wisconsin in Milwaukee, Wisconsin.

Between my third and fourth year of medical school, I obtained a scholarship and returned to the DC area to do research at the National Institute of Health. At this time, I worked in the Urologic Oncology branch and became even more fascinated with urologic oncology and the scientific process. After this experience, I knew that I wanted to follow in my father's footsteps as a urologic surgeon.

I am now living in Baltimore, Maryland, where I am privileged and thrilled to be a urology resident, completing my general surgery year at Johns Hopkins Hospital. I hope to not only become an excellent surgeon, but be able to continue asking questions and seeking their answers with the hope of making people healthier and happier. I also continue to be interested in how policy affects health care and an individual's health and would like to further explore this area.

3. Kaye, Maxine Joscelin

b: 28 July 1982, Minneapolis, MN, USA
occ: Law student, Columbia University
rec: Ballroom dance, travel
currently: New York, New York, USA

Figure 6.76.

Personal Story

I was born in Minneapolis, Minnesota, in July 1982 to two wonderfully busy parents. I grew up in Minnesota for most of my life, with a brief departure in Perth, Australia, where my dad was Chief of Urology at the University of Western Australia. Thanks to the great organizational skills of my father, I also picked up Australian citizenship during that time.

In high school I loved tennis and ballroom dancing. The crazy ballroom dancing dresses were mesmerizing, and my high school heart found it very romantic.

From high school in Minneapolis, I went to Barnard, an independent liberal arts college that is part of Columbia University in New York City. While in university, I continued ballroom dancing and also developed an interest in international relations and "saving the world." In my efforts to accomplish the latter, I held two internships at the United Nations, in which I learned that saving the world was not as easy as I first anticipated. In fact, the vehicle that I thought would lead to world salvation, the UN, was actually entirely incompetent and anti-Israel beyond reason. It was for this reason, I decided to work at the American Jewish Committee, a non-profit organization that among many other things, lobbies internationally on behalf of Israel. I worked for two years as the assistant to the executive director. This essentially meant traveling around the world, staying in lovely hotels, and meeting important people like presidents and foreign ministers, who, it turns out, are not as smart and all-knowing as I thought they would be. My time at AJC was unforgettable, but I wanted to go back to school, so after a beautiful summer in France, I returned to Columbia for law school, where I am in my third and final year.

I am working at Allen and Overy this summer, where I am working in capital markets and infrastructure project finance. I still have not forgotten about saving the world and hope that helping in infrastructure development and access to capital in the developing world will be at least a small step in the right direction.

Great-Great-Grandchildren of Johanna Graudan and Julius Holzberg: Peter Leyton Family (n=3)

1. Leyton, **Claudine Ann**

b: 9 Jan. 1973, N. Sydney, Australia
m: Brian Anthony Larkham, 30 Aug. 1997, Penrith, Australia
currently: Newcastle, NSW, Australia

Figure 6.77.

2. Leyton, **Mark Patrick**

b: 18 Dec. 1975, Johannesburg, S. Africa
occ: Air conditioning technician
currently: Newcastle, NSW, Australia

Figure 6.78.

3. Leyton, **Andrew Bernard**

b: 4 Aug. 1979, S. Africa
occ: Mechanic
currently: Sydney, Australia

Figure 6.79.

Great-Great-Grandchildren of Johanna Graudan and Julius Holzberg: Russel Jackson Family (n=2)

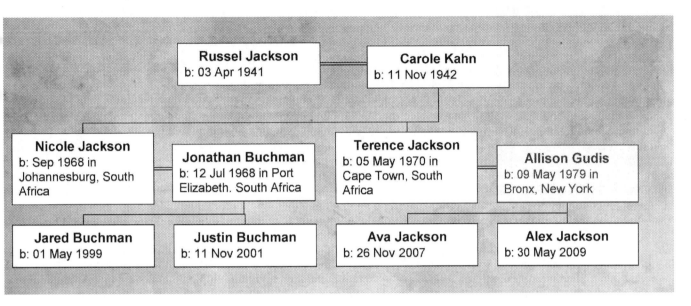

Figure 6.80. Russel Jackson Family

1. Jackson, **Nicole**

Figure 6.81.

b: Sept. 1968, Johannesburg, S, Africa
m: Jonathan Buchman
currently: Boston, Massachusetts, USA

2. Jackson, **Terence**

b: 5 May 1970, Johannesburg, S, Africa
occ: Periodontist
m: Allison Gudis
currently: Stamford, Connecticut, USA

Figure 6.82.

Personal Story

Terence S. Jackson, D.M.D, M.A., received his dental degree as well as his Certificate in Periodontology from Tufts University. He is Board-Certified by the American Academy of Periodontlogy and is also the recipient of the Kaufman Fellowship Award, which enabled him to study the effects of periodontal disease on the concentration of adhesion molecules in tissue. Prior to entering the field of dentistry, Dr. Jackson devoted four years to cardiovascular research at Boston University School of Medicine, where he earned a Masters in Biological Science. He also holds a B.S. in Business Administration. Dr. Jackson is a Diplomat of the American Board of Periodontology and is active in the Connecticut Periodontal Society, American Dental Association, and Connecticut Dental Society.

Great-Great-Grandchildren of Johanna Graudan and Julius Holzberg: Avril Jackson Family (n=3)

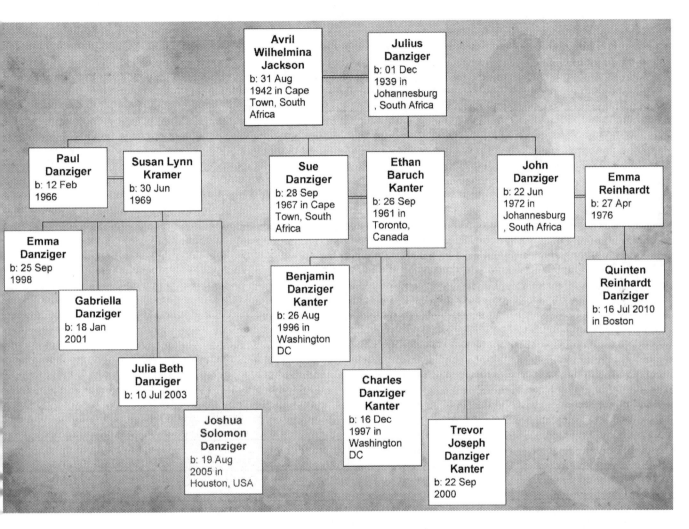

Figure 6.83. Avril Jackson Family

1. Danziger, **Paul**

b: 12 February 1966, Johannesburg, S. Africa
m: Susan Lynn Kramer
occ: Lawyer
rec: Playwright

Figure 6.84.

I recently wrote a screenplay, based on my true life experience, which is being made into a full-length Hollywood movie called "Retractable (aka Vanish Point)."

2. Danziger, **Susan**

b: 28 Sept. 1967, Cape Town, S. Africa
m: Ethan Baruch Kanter
occ: Specialist physician
currently: Garrett Park, Maryland, USA

Figure 6.85.

3. Danziger, **John**

b: 22 June 1972, Johannesburg, S. Africa
m: Emma Reinhardt
occ: Nephrologist
rec: Gardening, pottery

Figure 6.86.

Personal Story

I emigrated from South Africa to Houston at age five. I left Houston after high school for higher education, attending University of Pennsylvania for college, Cambridge University in England for graduate school, and the University of Texas for medical school. Currently, I am a nephrologist at Beth Israel Deceaconess Medical Center/Harvard Medical School, where I divide my time between clinical care, research, and teaching.

I married in 2009 to Emma Reinhardt in Boston, and we are expecting our first child this July (2010). We share our time between a small apartment in Boston, and an old farmhouse near the ocean, enjoying gardening, pottery, and long swims in the bay.

Great-Great-Grandchildren of Johanna Graudan and Julius Holzberg: Merril Jackson Family (n=2)

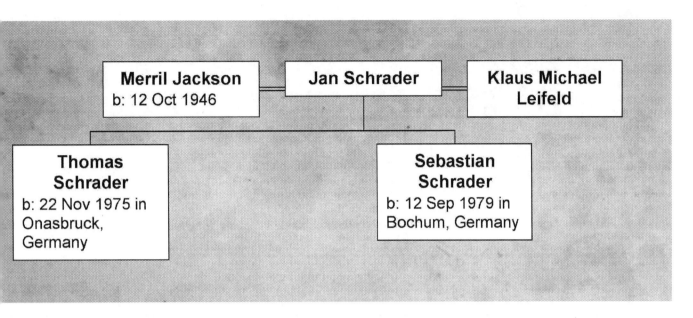

Figure 6.87. Merril Jackson Family

1. Schrader, **Thomas**

b: 22 Nov. 1975, Onasbruck, Germany
m. Maria Prekopva (divorced)
occ: Economics student
currently: Bochum, Germany

Figure 6.88.

Personal Story

By his mother Merril

Thomas worked four years in a small theater as a sound-engineer and is now studying economics; in fact, he is almost finished . . . he is solo again (unfortunately!). He was married to Maria, and after their divorce, he was together with a nice Russian lady.

2. Schrader, **Sebastian**

b: 12 Sept. 12 1979, Bochum, Germany
occ: Doctor
currently: Essen, Germany

Figure 6.89.

Personal Story

By his mother Merril

Sebastian is a doctor, specializing in internal medicine. He lives with his longstanding girlfriend Alma, who is an anaesthesiologist. He likes cooking and throwing big parties

Great-Great-Grandchildren of Johanna Graudan and Julius Holzberg:
Martin Jackson Family (n = 3)

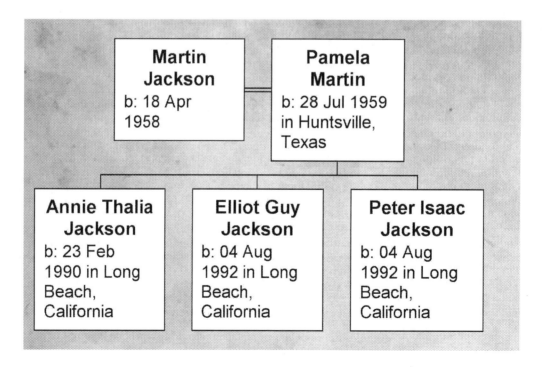

Figure 6.90. Martin Jackson Family

1. Jackson, **Annie Thalia**

b: 23 Feb. 1990

Figure 6.91.

2. Jackson, **Elliot Guy**

b: : 4 Aug. 1992 occ: Student

3. Jackson, **Peter Isaac**

b: : 4 Aug. 1992 occ: Student

Great-Great-Grandchildren of Johanna Graudan and Julius Holzberg:
Conrad Paul Lichtenstein Family (n=2)

1. Lichtenstein, **Munaye**

b: 16 Aug. 1966 occ: Student currently: London, UK

Figure 6.92.

2. Lichtenstein, **Daniel**

b: 12 Feb. 1998
occ: Student
currently: London, UK

Figure 6.93.

Great-Great-Grandchildren of Johanna Graudan and Julius Holzberg: Olivia Lichtenstein Family (n–2)

1. Humphreys, **Oscar**

b: 27 Aug. 1988, London, UK
occ: Student

Figure 6.94.

2. Humphreys, **Francesca**

b: 8 June 1993
occ: Student
rec: Singing, theatre, drama

Figure 6.95.

Great-Great-Great-Grandchildren

Great-Great-Great-Grandchildren of Johanna Graudan and Julius Holzberg (n=49, biologic=41):

1. Blumberg, **Gabrielle Dean**

b: 30 Nov 1984, Johannesburg, S. Africa
occ: Economics student, London School of Economics
rec: Travel, books, photography, live music, family
currently: London, UK

Figure 6.96.

Personal Story

I love economics and always have, in some way or another, immersed myself in its theories and practices. From New York University and a few years on a Foreign Exchange trading floor on Wall Street, I find myself now at the London School of Economics, studying economics and public policy for international development. During my summer break, I'm off to Bolivia for a few months to work with the local government to analyze some of their development programs.

Traveling, reading, photography, and hanging out with my family and friends are some of my favorite things. I also love going to see and hear live music (I keep every ticket stub of every show I've ever been to) and watching good films.

2. Blumberg, **Jessica Toni**

b. 31 March, White Plains, New York, USA
occ: Marketing and management For my mothers' interior design practice
rec: Basketball, family, friends, travel
currently: New York

Figure 6.97.

Personal Story

I graduated from the Leonard N. Stern School of Business at New York University in May 2009 with a double major in marketing and management. I'm currently working with my mom in interior design, after a short stint at a boutique public relations agency. Basketball will forever be a passion for me, and I now play on a team with a bunch of friends in New York City. I love summers, the beach, going out with friends, spending time with my family, traveling (I just finished up a ten-day road trip of a lifetime with my dad, from Santé Fe to San Francisco), and I have an extreme guilty pleasure for reality television!

3. Braune, **Isabella**

b: 24 Nov. 2000, Amsterdam, Holland

4. Braune, **Savannah**

b: 9 Aug. 2003, Amsterdam, Holland

5. Buchman, **Jared**

b: 1 May 1999, Boston, Massachusetts, USA

Figure 6.98.

6. Buchman, **Justin**

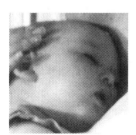

b: 11 Nov. 2001, Boston, Massachusetts, USA

Figure 6.99.

7. Buhai, **Zachary**

8. Buhai, **Jade**

b: 16 Nov. 2006, Johannesburg, S. Africa

9. Buhai, **Matt Gabriel**

Figure 6.100.

10. Buhai, **Ethan Judd**

b: 20 Aug. 2009, Johannesburg, S. Africa

Figure 6.101.

11. Danziger, **Emma**

b: 25 Sept. 1998, Houston, Texas, USA

Figure 6.102.

12. Danziger, **Gabriella**

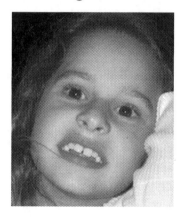

b: 18 Jan. 2001, Houston, Texas, USA

Figure 6.103.

13. Danziger, **Julia Beth**

b: 10 July 2003, Houston, Texas, USA

Figure 6.104.

14. Danziger, **Joshua Solomon**

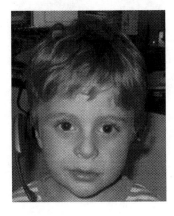

b: 19 Aug. 2005, Houston, Texas, USA

Figure 6.105.

15. Danziger, **Quinten Reinhardt**

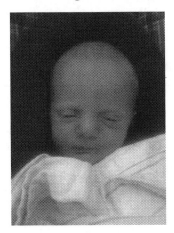

b: 16 July 2010, Boston, Massachusetts,USA

Figure 6.106.

16. Ender, **Matthiasis Noriskin**

b: 13 June 2000, Jhb, S. Africa

Figure 6.107.

17. Ender, **Alexa Noriskin**

b: 24 March 20005, Jhb, S. Africa

Figure 6.108.

18 Gardy, **Kate Alexandra**

b: 26 Feb. 1993, London, UK
occ: Student
rec: Sports, people, art, drama, music, languages, new places

Figure 6.109.

Personal Story

I grew up in the vibrant grey city of London and went to a Jewish primary school, Akiva. Loved the bustle of urban life and the cold, crisp mornings laced with cherry blossoms of early London spring. I spent the first ten years of my life in the UK and was fortunate enough to get a taste of various foreign lands from a young age. Definitely developed a love of traveling ☺. Moved to Plettenberg Bay, S. Africa, at the beginning of 2003—South Africa being the birth place of my parents.

Nothing could have been better than spending the rest of my childhood and teenage years in the land of sun and spirit; certainly brought a whole new dynamic to my life. I am a very artistic person; I love to paint, sing, dance, act, play the piano, and be creative in any way possible. I like to think I see beauty in the simplicity of life—I appreciate nature and the outdoors. I am rather laid back and live life at my own slow pace. I enjoy sports, people, art, drama, music, languages, new places, nail polish, and PEACE and Love.

19. Gardy, **Olivia Rebecca**

b: 14 Jan. 1996, London, UK
occ: Student
rec: Sports, music

Figure 6.110.

Personal Story

At the age of seven I moved to Plettenberg Bay. While living in London I attended Akiva, a lovely Jewish day school. In South Africa I went to Plettenberg Bay Primary School where I really blossomed and learned many things, especially about myself—things that I never would have experienced in the UK. For example, sports. I absolutely adore my sports and would totally not be able to live without it. I play hockey, football, tennis, netball, water polo, athletics, swimming, nippers (life-saving), adventure racing, skiing, cycling, surfing, and I am always willing to try anything new. I am also hugely interested in music. I love to play the guitar and listen to music. I am the kind of person who puts herself to the challenge and I am vibrant, outgoing, and always ready to have a jol!

20. Gardy, **Adam Antony**

b: 30 Dec. 1990, Johannesburg, S. Africa
occ: Pre-med student
rec: Sports, especially rowing

Figure 6.111.

Personal Story

Moved to Rye, New York, when I was five years old, where I lived for six years before moving to Rochester, New York. I played competitive basketball and baseball, until a fracture of the hip prevented any further contact sport. I took up rowing and became captain of Brighton Rowing Club in my senior year, winning a silver at the State Championships and numerous gold, silver, and bronze medals at regional regattas; but the highlight was rowing in the Head of the Charles Regatta in Boston—the biggest regatta in the world.

Last year I was accepted to The George Washington University in DC. I was fortunate enough to make the rowing team and had a successful year. I pledged in a Fraternity, Pi Kappa Alpha, and was appointed to the Community Service Chair. In my freshman year I was placed on the Scholar Athletes Dean's List and I'm really looking forward to continuing with my sophomore year as a pre-med student.

I hope to succeed in the field of orthopedics, or perhaps follow my great-grandfather's steps in radiology.

21. Gardy, **Michael Tomas**

b: 10 Jan. 1992, Johannesburg, S. Africa
occ: University student
rec: Sports, collecting

Figure 6.112.

Personal Story

I spent my early years in Rye, New York—always fascinated by all animals, bugs, and ocean life. I loved fishing and exploring. I moved to Rochester, New York, in fifth grade. I enjoyed playing football, basketball, and baseball before a serious knee injury put me out of competitive sports for almost two years. With the aid of a serious knee brace, I was able to train and make it back on the varsity basketball team.

I feel very close to my South African heritage and loved traveling to South Africa and volunteering in the bush and at a township school with my brother, Adam. I love excitement and have bungee jumped off the highest bridge in the world (Bloukrans, South Africa). I collect and trade in Nike SB sneakers and collect Coke memorabilia. I was counselor at the JCC summer camp, where I was honored with the top counselor award.

I will be attending University of Maryland as a freshman and hope to pursue a career in the engineering field.

22. Goldman, **Anna**

b: 16 Jan. 1985, Mpika, Zambia
occ: Architect, specializing in urban design
currently: Cape Town

Figure 6.113.

23. Goldman, **Maya Scott**

b: 21 June 1987, London, UK
occ: Teacher
currently: Toulouse, France

Figure 6.114.

24. Hamburger, **Samuel Shane**

b: 9 Dec. 2008, Johannesburg, S. Africa

25. Jackson, **Ava**

b: 26 Nov. 2007, USA

26. Jackson, **Alex**

b: 30 May 2009, USA

27. Jacob, **Hannah**

Figure 6.115.

28. Jacob, **Jamie**

Figure 6.116.

29. Jacob, **Joshua**

Figure 6.117.

30 Jacob, **Oliver**

Figure 6.118.

31. Jacob, **Natasha**

Figure 6.119.

32. Jacob, **Phoebe**

Figure 6.120.

33. Kallmeyer, **Olivia**

b: 28 June 2001, Boston, Massachusetts, USA

Figure 6.121.

34. Kallmeyer, **Sophia**

b: 10 May 2003, Boston, Massachusetts, USA

Figure 6.122.

35. Kallmeyer, **Benjamin Johannes**

b: 27 May 2010, Phoenix, Arizona, USA

Figure 6.123.

36. Kanter, **Benjamin Danziger**

b: 26 Aug. 1996, Washington DC, USA

Figure 6.124.

37. Kanter, **Charles Danziger**

b: 16 Dec. 1997, Washington DC, USA

Figure 6.125.

38 Kanter, **Trevor Joseph Danziger**

b: 22 Sept. 2000, Washington DC, USA

Figure 6.126.

39. Larkham, **Matthew Brian**

b: 2 Dec. 2000, Penrith, NSW, Australia

Figure 6.127.

40. Larkham, **Mya-Grace**

b: 24 July 2003, Penrith, NSW, Australia

Figure 6.128.

41. Lieberman, **Jackson Spira**

b: 31 Jan. 2009, New York, New York, USA

Figure 6.129.

42. Mann, **Aaron Saul**

b: 1 Sept. 1997, Toronto, Canada

Figure 6.130.

43. Mann, **Rachel Keryn**

b: 12 Jan. 2000, Toronto, Canada

Figure 6.131.

44. Mann, **David Josef**

b: 5 Nov. 2001, Toronto, Canada

Figure 6.132.

45. Morrison, **Thomas**

Figure 6.133.

46. Morrison, Analise

Figure 6.134.

47. Noriskin, **Elle**

b: 6 June 2008, Vancouver, Canada

Figure 6.135.

48. Spira, **Matthew Josef**

b: 7 April 2006, Johannesburg, S. Africa

Figure 6.136.

49. Spira, **Gabriel Ariah**

b: 28 Nov. 2008, Johannesburg, S. Africa

Figure 6.137.

CHAPTER 7

European Graudans
(Two Families: Moritz Graudan and Rocha Graudan)

Family 1. The Founding Father

Figure 7.1. **Gravestone of Moritz Graudan**

b: 29 Aug. 1856, Probably in Panevezys, Lithuania
m: Flora
occ: Doctor
d: 7 Aug. 1922, Libau, Latvia

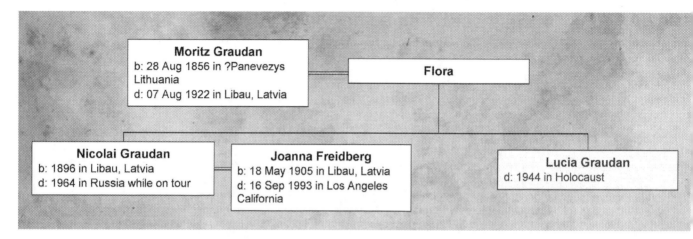

Figure 7.2. Children of Moritz Graudan

1. Graudan, **Nicolai (Kolya)**

b: 1896, Libau, Latvia
m: Joanna Freidberg
d: 1964, probably California, USA
occ: Concert cellist

Figure 7.3.

Story and Memories

See Appendix 2

Strings magazine, May/June 2001, No. 94

"Who Was That Guy, Anyway?" By Jeffrey Solow

Russian Nicolai Graudan (1896–1964) followed Piatigorsky as solo cellist of the Berlin Philharmonic. Germany under the Nazis became untenable, so Graudan went to London and on to the US, playing principal with the Minneapolis Symphony before relocating to Los Angeles. Graudan taught at the Aspen Festival and the Music Academy of the West in Santa Barbara, and joined Primrose's Festival Quartet. (And his wife, Joanna, taught many of my pianist friends.)

Response from Jeffrey Solow to Email I (Keith) sent him:

Dear Keith:

My mother, a violinist, knew Nicolai in LA and I knew Johanna—many of
my friends studied piano with her. Most notable among those students is
Mona Golabek, who has a popular radio program on Romantic Composers. Mona
may have a website. She lives in West Los Angeles.

From Mort Levin:

May 2010

Dear Jean Michel, thanks for the recording. Both Nicolai and his wife Joanna performed in Lorain,
Ohio, in the late fourties/early fifties when I was a child. They stayed, I believe, at our home, and we
visited with them In LA. Last time I saw Nicolai perform was when I was in law school in Ann Arbor.
So, Jean, you are bringing back memories of years gone by. Thanks again, Mort

From Ruth Levin:

July 2010

I included articles about Kolya Graudan, who I knew very well. I was the only relative other than his
wife Hansi at the memorial service for him.

**From Legacy, Vol. 5 (2), 1995 (Publication of the Jewish Community Foundation of Los Angeles; With
Permission):**

"Musicians Joanna and Nicholai Graudan Dedicate Legacy for a Jewish Future"

Figure 7.4. Nicholai and Joanna Graudan

An eye-to-eye confrontation between her husband, the first cellist of the Berlin Philharmonic Orchestra, and Adolf Hitler forced Joanna and Nicholai Graudan into a life-saving flight from Nazi Germany in the 1930s.

That experience, combined with the executions of her father, mother, sister, and sister-in-law during the Holocaust, and the opportunity to watch Israel grow on nearly annual visits, moved Mrs. Graudan to leave a nearly $25,000 bequest to the United Jewish Fund (UJF) Endowment Fund for the future support of the Jewish community.

Through gifts, such as Mrs. Graudan's, the income from the UJF Endowment Fund has become the largest single contribution to the UJF campaign, totaling $1.16 million in 1994.

Born in the Baltic town of Libau, Latvia, Mrs. Graudan fell in love with the piano as a young child. Despite the difficulties of life in Russia, she studied the piano and eventually went to Berlin, where she graduated from the Hochshule fuer Musik with honors.

Her husband, Nicholai Graudan, also grew up in Libau where they met years after each had gone to Berlin. Mr. Graudan studied cello at the St. Petersburg Conservatory and became first cellist for the Berlin Philharmonic Orchestra. Just prior to the final concert of the 1935 season, the conductor announced that Hitler would be attending, and the musicians would be required to salute him. Although Graudan said he could not do so, the conductor attempted to persuade him not to take the gesture so seriously. When the moment arrived, Graudan, as first cellist, was closest to the audience. He found himself face-to-face with Hitler, unable to raise his arm for the salute.

Two days later, the Graudans, with as much money as they could carry in a toothpaste tube, locked the door of the Berlin apartment and left for London, where he had a cousin. After a difficult two and a half years, they sailed on the Queen Mary for New York with a generous loan from their friend, Sir Anthony Rothschild, and the essential immigration papers signed by relatives in Brooklyn.

In 1945, telegram broke the news they had feared: only a sister-in-law and a niece had survived the Holocaust. Moved by the desire to visit relatives who had immigrated to Tel Aviv years before the war and to support the fledgling State of Israel by performing concerts and touring, the Graudans came to Israel in 1950.

"It's difficult for me to describe how deeply we were involved emotionally in the birth of Israel and the consciousness that there finally is a place on earth which the persecuted Jews—not only of Germany—can call their own country." Mrs. Graudan wrote later, "It was an overwhelming experience of hope and joy . . . the feeling of reverence, gratitude, and being part of it when we stepped on the soil of Israel."

Professionally, the Graudans were hailed as "clearly exquisite musicians" by the New York Herald Tribune. Mr. Graudan was a cellist for the Metropolitan Opera, served five years as first cellist for the Minneapolis Symphony, and won praise from conductor Arturo Toscanini. Together, the Graudans performed on strenuous concert tours that included New York, Chicago, Los Angeles, the Library of Congress in Washington DC, and various universities. They helped to establish the Aspen, Santa Fe, and Ojai music festivals. In 1949, they moved to Pacific Palisades where Mrs. Graudan taught music and later joined the University of Southern California music faculty and Mr. Graudan performed with the Festival Quartet, wrote and edited musical articles and books, and taught students. In 1966, they visited Russia again. On this trip, Mr. Graudan, who had been in declining health for a number of years, passed away.

"We no longer have the musical talents of Joanna and Nicholai Graudan with us," observed Stuart D. Buchalter, Foundation president. "But through Mrs. Graudan's generous bequest, we have an expression of the Graudan's generous and courageous spirit alive through the legacy they have left to our Jewish community in Los Angeles."

2. Graudan, **Lucia**

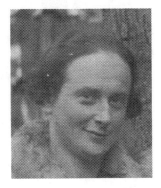

b: Libau, Latvia
d: 1944 in Holocaust

Figure 7.5.

Personal Comment: By Jean Michel Linois June 2008

Lucia Graudan was married and killed in 1944, apparently. Andre's belief is that she and her husband stayed in Berlin during WWII. Lucia was a fine musician, like her brother Nicolai. Ruth will tell you more from her grandma's diary dated 1928 when she visited Libau and spent time with her family: Nicolai, Lucia, Dina, and Rocha and husband Samuel. I got to read it and made copies: terribly moving.

* * *

The Founding Couple: Rocha and Samuel

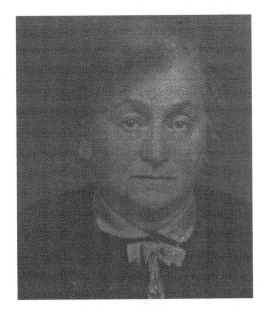

Figure 7.6. **Rocha Graudan**

[illegible]	[illegible]	[illegible]
399	FREIMANS, Ernests Ernesta dēls un Vera Ernesta meita un ŠTOLCERS, Katrīne Ernesta meita, rokdarbu veikals zem f-as „E. Freimans"	Graudu 48
400	FREIMANS, Jānis Davida dēls, koloniāl preču veikals zem f-as „J. C. Freimans"	Petera 9
401	FREIMANS, Jānis Davida dēls un Antonija, kafijas lieltirgotava, zem f-as „J. C. Freimans"	Bāreņu 35
402	FREIMANS, Karlis, pārtikas preču veikals	Čaoļu 9
403	FREIMANS, Mārtiņš Iizes dēls, veclietu veikals	Siena 8
404	FRĪDBERGS, Anele, pārtikas preču veikals	Aleksandra 78
405	FRĪDBERGS, Davids Moza dēls, vīnu tirgotava	Peldu 11
406	FRĪDBERGS, Rahele-Freide, pārtikas preču veikals	Toma 28
407	FRĪDLANDS, Ida Zamueļa meita, modes preču veikals	Ludviķa 9
408	FRĪDLENDERS, Zamuels Abrama dēls krāsns podu tirgotava	Zāģeru lauk. 16

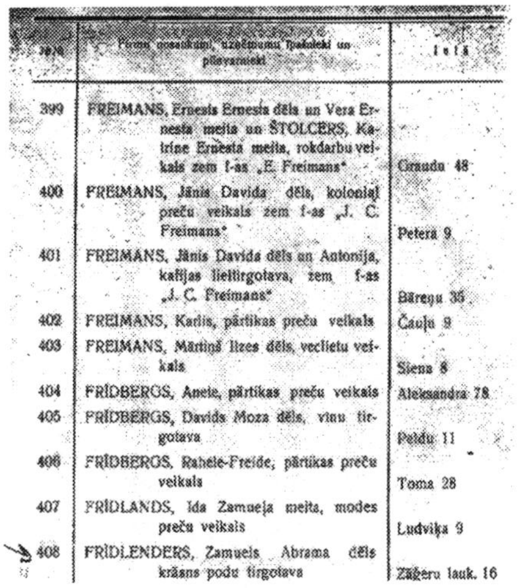

Figure 7.7. **Samuel Friedlander**

www.shtetlinks.jewishgen.org/Liepajalat/Ft30p028.jpg

b: 19 Jun 1861, Panevezys, Lithuania;
d: After August 1941, Libau, Latvia during Shoah;

b: 1854
d: 1 Jun 1938, Libau, Latvia

Personal Story and Memories

Not sure exactly when Rocha died. She was still alive in August 1941, as she was listed in the late August 1941 census. As below, from Edward Anders email, Rocha may have been killed in September/October 1941 during an "*aktion* for eliminatiion of old Jews" or she may have been liquidated at Skede. (Appendix 3)

PERSON SHEET (www.liepajajews.org)

Name: Rocha Friedländer
Birth: June 19, 1861. There is, however, some discrepancy. From her marriage record she was stated as being twenty-five years old in 1895 and would, therefore, have been born in 1870.
Death: 1941, Liepāja
Address before the war: 11 Uliha St., Top Floor, Apt 6
Address 29 6 1941: Toma St. 38, Apt 3.
Occupation: Unemployed (sick)
Flags: Killed
Spouse: Samuel Friedlander was a widower from Pilten when they married. He was born c. 1855 and was thirty-nine and three-quarters years old at the time of his marriage to Rocha.
Children: Jenny (1900–1941)

Email from Jean Michel Linois:

April 2009

My dear cousins,

Some weeks ago, I watched an interview of this Gentleman, M. ANDERS, one of the rare survivors of LIBAU's Jewish community in 1945, who now lives in the US. He dedicated his life to documenting Jewish life in Libau and putting together all testimonies that may help us all regain as much knowledge of the fate of our beloved lost ones.

I dared writing to him since we never really got much information about the fate of my great-grandmother Rocha and of my grandaunt Jenny.

I wasn't really expecting an answer and here is what I got (message and attachments), including that part about Kolya and Hansi GRAUDAN.

It is amazing and still there is so much left unknown. I send you my deepest love and share of the sorrow, as we just commemorated Holocaust victims generically.
Jean Michel

From Edward Anders:

April 2009

Dear Mr. Linois-Linkovskis:

Thank you for your kind words. Although I lost twenty-five members of my family (only my mother and I survived), I suffered less during the Holocaust than did other Liepāja Jews, and I therefore feel obligated to do something for remembrance. Only 20 precent of their names were known by Yad Vashem in 1998, which would have pleased Hitler.

Rocha and Jenny Friedlaender definitely were not killed in June 1941. Most claims of killings in Latvia before arrival of the Germans are spurious, except for a few in Riga. Both women are listed in the late August 1941 census, Rocha as sick and unemployed but Jenny as working for Germans. That information is on my website: www.liepajajews.org

There is much more information on the *Person Sheet*. From any family card, click on the bold-faced name (blue) at the top of the family card. That will bring up a *Person Sheet* containing all the known information about that person. Click the numbers in parentheses to find where each piece of information comes from.

Rocha may have been killed in September/October 1941 during an "*aktion* for eliminatiion of old Jews." But that *aktion* spared a fair number; both my grandmothers survived until the December massacre. Jenny may have survived that massacre if her German bosses gave her one of the coveted pink slips, but they were intended only for essential workers.

I am attaching a list of all Jews who lived at Toma 38 (Figure EU 7.8). Unfortunately, very few of them survived and most of them would be dead by now. I am also sending you an article about wartime events in Liepāja (see below).

Kind regards, Edward Anders

Last Name	First & Mid Name	Birth Date	Birth Place
Aronstamm	Cilla	24 6 1913	Liepaja
Aronstamm	Gutman	4 5 1911	Grobina
Dagowitz	Ida-Geso	1890	__ LT
Dagowitz	Jakob	8 9 1939	__ LT
Dagowitz	Meier-Michl	11 4 1882	Breslau/DE
Dagowitz	Musja	1 6 1941	Liepaja
Dagowitz	Naum	16 11 1907	Liepaja
Dagowitz	Reise	10 10 1908	__ LT
Dagowitz	Riva	1910	Liepaja
Dagowitz	Vladimir	abt 1915	
Friedländer	Jenny	1 1 1900	Liepaja
Friedländer	Rocha	19 6 1861	Panevezys/LT
Gutman	Benno	1894	__ LT
Gutman	Seile	28 10 1898	__ LT
Harchurin	Lina	5 5 1895	Grobina
Harchurin	Mendel	9 9 1901	Liepaja
Harchurin	Sulamit	21 7 1931	Liepaja
Jakobson	Leib	9 8 1912	Ventspils
Jakobson	Scheine	20 1 1915	Liepaja
Katz	Berta	23 10 1885	__ LT
Katz	Wolf	17 2 1918	Liepaja
Klempner	David	19 5 1865	Talsi
Klempner	Hena	1874	Sabile
Klompus	Haze	1876	__ LT
Lewin	Hilde	25 4 1929	Liepaja
Lewin	Mirjam	27 12 1906	Skuodas/LT
Lewin	Salomon	1896	__ LT
Liebermann	Klara	10 10 1875	Liepaja
Michelson	Rosa	6 1 1866	Palanga/LT
Neuburger	Jemina	28 2 1891	Liepaja
Neuburger	Josef	29 8 1891	Bauska
Padzorova	Olga	19 7 1908	__ SU
Schoffmann	Gute	1873	__ SU
Schoffmann	Hankel	1902	Liepaja
Schoffmann	Minna	14 12 1903	__ LT
Westermann	Rosa	18 6 1915	Liepaja
Westermann	Samuel	9 6 1912	Liepaja
Wulf	Ada	12 5 1886	Jelgava
Wulf	Namija	10 10 1863	Liepaja
Wulfsohn	Hane	1876	__ LT
Wulfsohn	Naftel	20 8 1910	Liepaja

Total: 41

Figure 7.8.   Residents of #38, Toma St. Libau, prior to the German invasion of Latvia, June 1941

"Jews in Liepāja/Latvia, 1941–45: A Database of Victims and Survivors"

Edward Anders (Burlingame, California, USA) and Juris Dubrovskis (Riga, Latvia).

From: Edward Anders' website: www.liepajajews.org. Used with permission.

Many Liepāja Jewish families and their friends were totally wiped out in the Holocaust, leaving nobody to remember their names. Thus, of the 6,500+ Liepāja Jews who perished in WWII, only about 1,500 have so far been recorded at Yad Vashem. Such oblivion would have pleased Hitler.

We began in 1998 to search for the names, recovered at least 93 percent, and have been listing them on this website. The methodology of this project has been described in an article in Holocaust and Genocide Studies. A memorial book was published in March 2001 and about 1,000 copies were sent at no charge to all Liepāja Jews (or descendants) whose addresses we knew and to about two hundred libraries and archives. The entire printing has been distributed, except for a few copies in Israel. The present (May 2008) revision of this website is likely to be the last.

Events of 1941–45.

About 7,100 Jews lived in Liepāja, Latvia, on 14 June 1941. (Our database contains 7,142 names, but several hundred are possible duplicates). About 208 were deported to the USSR that day, a few hundred fled to the USSR after Germany attacked the USSR on 22 June 1941, and most of the remaining ones were killed during the German occupation that began on 29 June 1941. Most men were shot during the summer and fall; at first near the lighthouse, then on the Naval Base, and from October 1941 on in the dunes of Shkede north of town. Women and children were largely spared until the big aktion of 14–17 December 1941, when 2,749 Jews were shot. (For further information, see pictures of the shootings, taken by the Security Police and secretly copied by survivor David Zivcon, and the account by historian Andrew Ezergailis). Killings continued in early 1942, and by the time the ghetto was established on 1 July 1942, only 832 Jews were left.

The ghetto was closed on 8 October 1943 when the survivors were taken to Riga. Young adults were generally spared, but in the next few months older people and women with children were killed locally or in Auschwitz. When the Red Army approached Riga in the summer of 1944, the survivors were sent to the Stutthof concentration camp near Danzig in several transports, from August to October 1944. Many died in the increasingly brutal conditions of this camp, especially on death marches in early 1945, and only 175 survived. Of the deportees and refugees to the USSR, many perished, but some three hundred survived. (Appendix 3)

Children of Rocha Graudan and Samuel Friedlander (n=3)

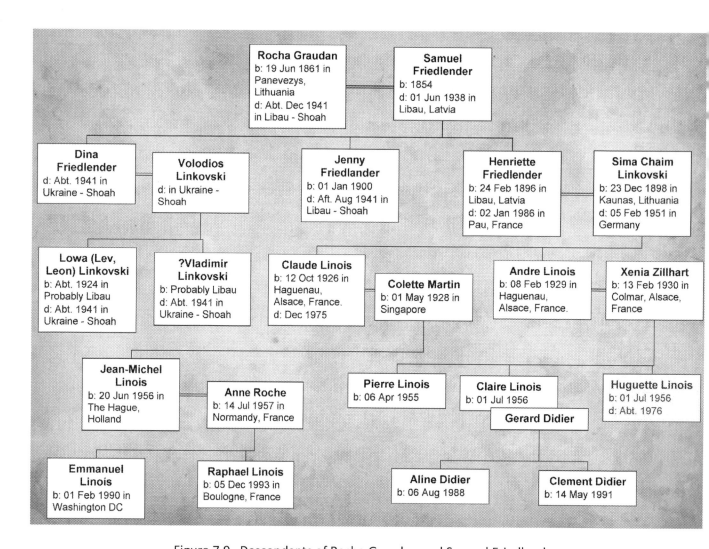

Figure 7.9. Descendants of Rocha Graudan and Samuel Friedlander

1. Friedlander, **Dina**

b: Probably Libau, Latvia
m: Volodios Linkovski
d: c. 1941 during Shoah in Ukraine

Figure 7.10.

Personal Story

From Jean Michel Linois (June 2008)

Dina Friedlaender married Sima Chaim Linkovski's brother Volodios (Vladimir) Linkovski. Indeed, two sisters, Henriette and Dina, married two brothers.

Dina and Volodios moved from the Baltic States and settled before WWII in Kharkov (Ukraine). I don't know why, though. They raised two boys (Vladimir and Leon), who must have been born circa 1930. Their fate and that of their children was that of the Jews of Ukraine. Probably not deported to extermination camps but executed in mass killings by Einsatzgruppen. (PS: I never quite understood why one of the sons was named after his father. Could it be that the father died during his wife's pregnancy? Not likely, though).

All four of them and Jenny and Rocha are now listed with a specific personal sheet in the Yad Vashem Shoah victim's database. I took care of that so their names are not forever lost.

2. Friedlander, **Henriette (Jettchen)**

> b: 24 Feb. 1896, Libau, Latvia
> m: Sima Chaim Linkovski
> d: 2 Jan. 1986, Pau, France

Figure 7.11.

Personal Story

From Jean Michel Linois (July 2008)

Henriette, my Grandma, would have been a great individual to interview. She went through so much in Russia during the early years of the communist regime!

She and my grandpa Sima married shortly before the February 1917 revolution. Grandpa, thanks to the possibility given to Jews to become officers of the Russian army as a result of the Kerenski regime, became a cadet (Military Corps of Engineers). He was in St. Petersburg when the October 1917 revolution broke out. Trapped in the Winter Palace with a bunch of Cadets, he managed to escape and later boarded a ship to Constantinople. There, he joined the French Foreign Legion in order to gain French citizenship. His goal was, at the end of his five-year contract, to be able to settle in France (Alsace), where one of his first cousins was established. Meanwhile, his wife, Henriette, was forced to stay in Russia (she studied dentistry in Voronej). She tore her papers that proved she was married (to an enemy of the Bolsheviks). In 1924, however, she paid tribute to Lenin's coffin. Shortly after, she was able to flee Russia and get back to independent Latvia. She then immigrated to France and remarried her husband under French civil Law. Both became French citizens, and my father was born in October 1926.

I'm trying to get details of grandpa's military carrier with the Foreign Legion: he fought in Syria, was stationed in Algeria . . .

In the course of the summer of 1934, Henriette Linkovski took her two boys (Claude and Andre) on a trip to Libau, where they met their Grandmother Rocha and Aunt Jenny. This was the last time all three of them met.

3. Friedlander, **Jenny**

b: 1 Jan. 1900, Libau, Latvia
m: Never
d: After Aug. 1941, in Libau during Shoah

Figure 7.12.

Memories

Not sure when Jenny died. She was still alive in August 1941 as she was listed in the late August 1941 census. She thus may have been killed in the December massacre at Skede or may even have survived to live in the ghetto. (See Appendix 3)

PERSON SHEET from www.liepajajews.org

Name: Jenny Friedländer
Birth: 1900 (?)
Death: abt 1941, Liepāja

Address: Before 29 6 1941, Ulicha 11–61,9
Address 29 6 1941, Toma 38–3
Occupation: Laborer, works for Germans
Alias/AKA: Jenny
Flags: Killed?
Mother: Rocha Friedländer (1861–1941)
Spouses: Unmarried

* * *

Grandchildren of Rocha Graudan and Samuel Friedlander (n=4)

1. Linkovski, **Lowa (Lev, Leon)**

> b: abt 1924, probably Libau
> d: abt 1941, during Shoah in Woronej, Ukraine

Figure 7.13.

2. Linkovski, (?) **Vladimir**

> b: ?, probably Libau
> d: abt 1941, during Shoah in Woronej, Ukraine

3. Linois (born Linkovski), **Claude**

> b: 12 Oct. 1926, Haguenau, Alsace, France
> m: Colette Martin
> occ: Engineer
> d: Dec. 1975

Figure 7.14.

Memories

From son, Jean Michel Linois

In 1962, Claude changed his name from Linkovski to Linois. He was an engineer and patent lawyer.

Born in Haguenau (Alsace), he later moved with his parents to Strasbourg. In 1939, his mother and his brother were evacuated to Rennes (Brittany); as the German troops invaded France, they were joined by his father down south in the "free zone," in the city of Pau. They all spent the war years in Pau. He attended the local high school, and met my mother Colette at the local music school where both were among the talented pianists. Right after the war, he went to Bordeaux to prepare for the competitive entry exams for engineering schools; he was admitted to the Grenoble Polytechnical School.

After graduating and upon return of my mother from New York City, where she spent six years, they both married and moved to the Netherlands. They lived there from 1953 to 1966.

Dad was a gifted musician, a very sensitive artist, and he had a talent for foreign languages: he was perfectly fluent in French, English, German, Russian, Spanish, and Dutch. Not very outspoken, certainly rich of spirituality, he would mostly enjoy a great book, a gentle hilly landscape, the quietness of family home, and playing chess. I was amazed at his immense knowledge of history. Never satisfied by a level of achievement, he tought me, leading by example, to aim for perfection.

We all believe he was an engineer by accident and that he would have made a great scholar in humanities or a concert pianist instead.

His life ended after a painful brain cancer in 1975.

4. Linois, **Andre**

b: 8 Feb. 1929, Haguenau, Alsace, France
m: Xenia Zillhart
occ: Engineer
currently: Marseilles, France

Figure 7.15.

Personal Story

By Jean Michel Linois

Andre was born approximately two and half years after his brother Claude and both boys grew up in Hagenau (Alsace) prior to locating, in the mid-thirties' to the nearby main city of Strasbourg, as their father, Sima, had been hired as an accounting clerk at the Municipal Public Transportation Authority. With war looming ahead, the family was evacuated to Rennes and later to Pau. Andre attended school in Pau while the family lived under harsh conditions under the German occupation of France. He was able to pursue higher education after the war in Bordeaux and Grenoble, following the path taken by his older brother Claude. He graduated from the same engineering school in Grenoble and married Xenia Zilhart, a second cousin on his father's side. She had been raised in a family who assimilated to the Alsation Protestant Culture.

Andre's professional life started in the civil engineering business, designing dams for the hydroelectric program of the French National Electric Grid. After several years he joined EDF (The Electric Grid Company), where he spent the rest of his career. He moved to many places (Marseilles, Perigeaux, Paris) and raised with Xenia their three children. Ever since he joined Scout troops as a teenager, his delight has been going outdoors, hiking mountain trails, and skiing. Although he was exposed to music and piano in his youth, along with Claude, at the Pau Conservatory (Music School), he did not nurture his musical skills in the same way as Claude, but wasnevertheless appreciative of opera.

Rough times came to Andre and Xenia as a string of family events accumulated in the mid-1970s. Andre and Xenia retired in Marseille.

* * *

Great-Grandchildren of Rocha Graudan and Samuel Friedlander (n=4)

1. Linois, **Jean Michel**

b: 20 June 1956, the Hague, Holland
m: Anne Roche
occ: Agronomist and economist, PhD in Geography. French High Representative for the Dead Sea-Red Sea Water Conveyance Project
rec: Family, running, hiking, cycling, cross-country skiing, Hebrew, Yiddish, clarinet player (Kletzmer). Languages: French, English, German, Spanish
currently: Paris, France

Figure 7.16.

Personal Story

My paternal grandparents (Sima and Henriette Linkovski) came from Russia and my grandmother spoke French with an exotic accent; my father (Claude) was born in Alsace, my mother (Colette) in Singapore; Dad's family was strictly limited to his mother, his brother (Walodia), and sister-in-law (Dina), also mysteriously blood-related to him, and their three children. I was born and raised as a single child in the Netherlands; my last name is Linois; I am definitely a Gallic Frenchman deeply rooted in the French *terroir*!

Come December 1975, my father's terminal illness left my mother and I in a dramatic state of loss. As a young adult, and earlier on as a teenager, I never dared question my parents about our family history, though they would on some occasions prompt me to consider that some kind of family secret was involved in the whole situation.

Dad was a loving and caring father but his stern attitude and secrecy would not be inviting for any question not spontaneously tabled for discussion; I could never have imagined him as a child; he had no past, or, more to the point, his past was buried in a world that wasn't in the realm that I was supposed to access; Mom was geared to action, not so much cultivating family ties beyond the most inner circle and she would not "lose time" in futile discussions about the past.

121

Early 1976, I need to establish official documents and am naturally required to ask Mom for the official family records that include birth certificates and wedding certificate of my parents'. What should I have expected? Not only my grandparents' name wasn't Linois but I myself wasn't born Linois.

A wonderworld had opened up with the promising flurry of foreign surnames and first names: Linkovskis, Friedlaender, Sima, Chaim, Iossef ... . and places (Kovno, Libau . . .) all lined up in the coldest fashion in which official documents display history and geography.

My quest for this hidden past, roots spreading to foreign lands and nourished by generations of living tradition and faith, was about to start. A most formidable voyage of over three decades of study to regain ownership, pride, and responsibility in what should have been transmitted most naturally to me bearing the tragic events that peppered the first half of the twentieth century in Middle Europa and beyond, in Europe as a whole.

Dear Sima Chaim, my late grandfather whose death predated by just a few years my own birth; dear Henriette-Jettchen-Mamita, my late grandmother who helped me recapture my Jewish Askhenazi heritage thanks to a few hints and waypoints, this adventure changed my life for good.

I am glad that your siblings, your parents, and other relatives whose names I could retrieve from oblivion are now part of a Yizkor that I care about. Those whom I could record for eternal rememberance at *Yad Vashem*: you will witness the final victory of life, of the Covenant at the Sinai, of the power of the Shema and resilience of God's People and humankind as a whole against barbaric Nazi crimes. Dear sons, Emmanuel and Raphael, may the eternal light (Ner Tamid) burn for your hearts and help you find your bearings in your adult life; may you always remember your blended heritage not in a state of confusion, relativism, indifference, or disdain. Your wealth is, for some substantial part, a fruit of a lineage of relatives whom you never met, whose lifes and values find mysterious channels to reach you beyond material borders in time and location. May you teach your own children, not to forget ever! This undertaking was important for me; its outcome is too powerful and meaningful not to be passed along (*Veshinantam lebeineikha*). I bless you, my dear sons.

A very special thought for my wife Anne who has supported me throughout the past quarter century and must have felt overloaded with my emotional excitement and whose welcoming of countless relatives into our "mishpakha" has been exceptional.

A loving and thankful recognition for Mom's acceptance of my "mutation" and of the destabilizing surge of Dad's relatives who were not supposed to exist in the first place!

On a personal basis I am interested in modern history and geopolitics. I am a longstanding amateur student of Jewish history and culture; a dedicated learner of Hebrew and Yiddish; and a clarinet player (kletzmer). I trained as an agronomist and economist, with a PhD in Geography. Later I graduated from the Ecole Nationale d'Administration (civil service academy analogous to the Kennedy School of Management). I pursued a career with international assignments in the public and private sectors: Intelsat (Washington D.C), diplomatic adviser to several Cabinet Members of the French Government (2002–2008). Currently I am the French High Representative for the Dead Sea-Red Sea Water Conveyance Project.

Last but not least, special recognition should be expressed to my dear cousin Keith Kaye, whose efforts to put together this impressive collective work made it possible, and for having linked the European and South African limbs of our family tree. I must also express my gratitude for my cousins Ruth Kalin and Morton Levin, who welcomed with enthusiasm the gathering of the European and American limbs of our Graudan tree.

Kol Hakavod! Congratulations!

Jean Michel LINOIS (LINKOVSKIS)

July 2010, Minneapolis (USA)

2. Linois, **Pierre**

b: 6 April 1955
occ: Engineer
rec: Reading, music, cooking
currently: Paris, France

Figure 7.17.

Personal Story

By Jean Michel Linois

Pierre was born as Henriette Linkovski's first grandchild. His schooling and higher education led him to graduate from the same engineering school as his father and uncle and to join the French Electric Power Grid as well. Pierre is single and a very avid reader and classic music amateur. Prior to a very daring mountain climbing accident in his early twenties Pierre was an accomplished mountaineer. He also developed greatly-appreciated cooking skills. The genealogic work initiated by several members of the family provided him with a wealth of information about his family background, which he enjoys very much.

3. Linois, **Claire**

b: 1 July 1956
m. Gerard Didier
occ: Engineer in town planning esp social housing
rec: Taiji Quan, cinema, theatre, music esp classic, jazz, French singers, reading French and foreign novels, therapies in personal development
currently: Lyon, France

Figure 7.18.

Personal Story

By Jean Michel Linois

Claire and twin sister Huguette grew up as two peas in a pod. Both brilliant students, they pursued different higher educations—Claire graduated from Civil Engineering and Urban Development School in Lyon and later married Gerard Didier, then became a professor at an engineering school. They raised their two children in Lyon. Claire developed an urge of a quest of the family origins in much the same timeframe as her first cousin, Jean Michel, that is in her mid-twenties, and discussed these matters with her grandmother Henriette in parallel with Jean Michel's own initial search for paternal family tradition and history.

She relishes the reconnection with relatives from overseas, and is thankful for the joint efforts to clarify the family history and story.

4. Linois, **Huguette**

b: 1 July 1956
d: abt Aug. 1978

Figure 7.19.

Personal Story

By sister Claire

My very loved sister, who chose to disappear, has left all the family very sad.

Great-Great-Grandchildren of Rocha Graudan and Samuel Friedlander (n=4)

1. Didier, **Aline**

b: 6 Aug. 1988
occ: Student in psychology and specialist in old growing
currently: Lyon, France (lives with two others girls in a flat)

Figure 7.20.

2. Didier, **Clement**

b: 14 May 1991, Bron, Rhône-Alpes, France
occ: Student in commercial and management
rec: In love with football and tennis
currently: France

Figure 7.21.

3. Linois, **Emmanuel (Manu)**

b: 1 Feb. 1990, Washington DC, USA
occ: Student at Collegiate Business School, ESG in Paris
rec: Guitar player and amateur composer. Languages: French, English, German
currently: Paris, France. Dual citizenship (French and US)

Figure 7.22.

Personal Story

I was born in Washington DC on a cold February morning. I can still picture the house and the neighborhood where I grew up, and met my first friends. Our family moved to France a couple years later and it was not until I was seven that I went back to where it all started.

I was raised bilingual and was confronted with multicultural atmospheres and backgrounds among my schoolmates from the International Junior High School in Sèvres, and with my friendships and relationships.

I picked up music on my own when I was twelve after several attempts from both my parents and my grandmother who wanted me to play the piano, as they felt I was talented for it. Colette (my father's mother) was a piano teacher and was set up to be a professional performer, while she attended Julliard School courses in her days. Music, and especially the guitar, have appealed to me and shaped my life ever since. It has been a vector through which I keep on connecting with people and players in another way than with words.

4. Linois, **Raphael (Raffi)**

b: 5 Dec. 1993, Paris, France
occ: Student
rec: Guitar, tennis, golf. Languages: French, English, German, Spanish
currently: Paris, France

Figure 7.23.

Personal Story

I was born in Paris, France, in December 1993, where my parents and brother had already been living for about six months. I was raised as a complete French boy, though my education included an "Anglo-Saxon" culture part. Indeed, my family had just returned from Washington DC, a sort of "Golden age" I'm still told about. Therefore, I'm the result of this strange cultural mix. Thanks to this, I learned a lot and got this kind of "foreigner's point of view" in my country. It had good aspects and bad ones. It mostly created some differences between me and my schoolmates, and it's the reason why I stopped attending this bilingual school I used to go to. From that moment, that is to say at the age of eight, I have developed my true French identity, facing my parents' disappointment. I went to the St. Joseph School, a private Catholic school that went along with my Christian education.

At the age of eleven, I took example on my elder brother Manu and began learning the guitar, which I still play. I also played a lot of tennis.

I had never done a great job in school, until 2008, and the beginning of high school. While entering high school, I faced reality, which means hard work. Besides, I suddenly realized how bad our world was going and how Man was sabotaging Mother Nature, partly because of my dad's involvement in the French Ministry of the Environment. This explains my sudden motivation to get out of school as fast and as well as possible so as to start my part in "changing the world." This statement might sound really ambitious, but it's a true motivation. I'm in my last year of high school and I now plan to do a business school, whether in France or abroad, and then try a master in international relations. But my choice isn't made yet.

These last years have been really amazing concerning "family discoveries." It starts off with our dad coming up one day with the will of finding back his "hidden family." Then starts an incredible story: cousins appeared one after the other, filling up the blanks in the family's genealogy.

We are now visiting the Kaye family in Minneapolis—some extremely nice cousins. I'm writing this little biography for Keith, whom I respect very much and who has done such a good job with this book.

Finally, I've discovered, mostly thanks to Keith, one of my greatest passions: water skiing! Thanks again!

CHAPTER 8

American Graudans
(Sarah and Her Descendents)

The Founding Couple

Figure 8.1. Sarah Graudan

b: 11 Jun 1871, Libau, Latvia;

d: 2 May 1950, Lorain,Ohio USA;

Figure 8.2. Julius Isaac Quasser

b: 25 Jan, 1868, Libau, Latvia

d: 1933 in Portsmouth,Ohio

Memories

By granddaughter Ruth Levin (See Appendix 2)

Grandma Sarah was a tutor of the Quasser family four daughters and married their older brother Issac in Libau on July 5, 1894. She lost two sons in infancy and then had Adolf in 1900 and Judith on April 24, 1902. Moved to Portsmouth, Ohio, in abt 1912. Grandma Sarah loved playing piano and played duets with my mom, Judith. She played Bridge, made fabulous Jello molds, read, loved listening to classical music and attending concerts, movies, lectures, observed Judaism and attended services. After her son's death she moved in with us.

    Mom and Grandma were extremely close. She spent much effort to locate family in Europe after the Shoah and cried so hard when one niece was found through the Red Cross. She was Jean Michel's grandmother. I have much of her beautiful embroidery work on tablecloths and decorative linen pieces, as well as blankets she knitted. Swimming in the Baltic Sea or Lake Erie was a huge favorite of hers also.

Children of Sarah Graudan and Julius Isaac Quasser (n=2)

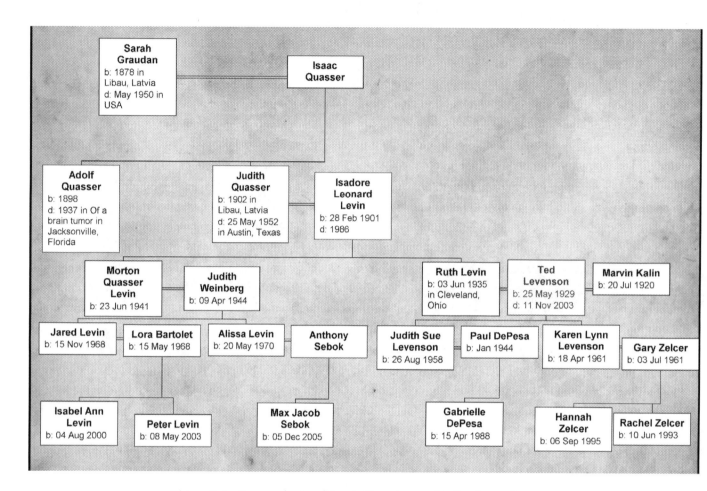

Figure 8.3. Descendants of Sarah Graudan and Julius Isaac Quasser

1. Quasser, **Adolf**

Figure 8.4.

b: 1900
d: 1937, Jacksonville, Florida, USA
occ: Doctor

130

2. Quasser, **Judith**

b: 24 April 1902, Libau, Latvia
d: 25 May 1952, Austin, Texas, USA
m: Isadore Levin, MD, May 28, 1932

Figure 8.5.

Memories

By daughter Ruth Levin

My mother was a school teacher prior to marriage and then a substitute teacher. She was actively involved in Judiasm, Hadassah Sisterhood President, AAUW active member, and Temple Choir director; she played piano, studied music, and had a beautiful voice; she was very cultured and well read. She was most loving, kind, giving, and always helping others; her family came first throughout her life. She enjoyed swimming, theater, lectures, traveling, bridge games, and entertaining. A woman of valor, indeed.

* * *

Grandchildren of Sarah Graudan and Julius Isaac Quasser (n=2)

1. Levin, **Ruth**

b: 3 June 1935, Cleveland, Ohio, USA
m: Ted Levenson (divorced)
m: Marvin Kalin
occ: Taught drama and speech in high school, para-professional counselor
currently: Encino, California, USA

Figure 8.6.

Personal Story

Theater, music, dance, sports fan of Los Angeles Lakers Basketball Team, docent at Skirball Cultural Center, Bnai Mitzvah for seventieth birthday, traveling everywhere, step-mother, and in love with all our seven grandchildren, relax at the beach every summer, and enjoy celebrating all Jewish Holy Days with family.

Personal Comment

By Jean Michel Linois

Thanks to her heart of gold and inspiring energy, Ruthie helped us reconnect with the US side of the family. Ruthie produced a uniquely moving evidence of the closeness of our family ties in spite of the six decades of apparent oblivion following the trauma of the shoah. She showed me her necklace that had been crafted around the stone offered by my grandmother Henriette (Jettchen) to Ruth's mother, Judith, in 1945.

The emotional family reunion in Los Angeles in the summer of 2007 was master-minded by Ruthie and will remain a major milestone in my life. Thanks to her, the torch has been handed over to the next generations. May the Eternal bless her for her kindness and love!

She and husband Marv adopted us right away and we are deeply greatful to them. She also helped me relate further to my religious roots.

2. Levin, **Morton Quasser**

> b: 23 June 1941
> m: Judith Weinberg
> occ: Lawyer. real estate developer
> currently: Cleveland, Ohio, USA

Figure 8.7.

Personal Story

Judy and I traveled to Libau, Latvia, and to Trishkey, Lithuania, in July 2005 to locate the home of my grandparents and the location where my mother, I believe, was born. We saw their home in Libau, and found the grave of the brother, Maurice, in Libau. Of course, we were also taken to the mass grave of all of those killed by the Nazis on June 22, 1941.

Judy and I have lived in Cleveland for forty-two years. I was an attorney and in the real estate business for a few years with uncles, and then I opened my own office and joined with a few others in a law practice. That led me to the real estate business full time for more than twenty-five years. I am still working at it, with a staff downtown of eight, and about forty people in the field, mostly in multi-family apartments, some industrial warehouses, and vacant land development.

Great-Grandchildren of Sarah Graudan and Julius Isaac Quasser (n=4)

1. Levin, **Jared**

b: 15 Nov. 1968
m: Lora Bartolet, MD
occ: Orthopedic surgeon
rec: Sports, golf, temple, and Harvard alumni groups
currently: Cleveland, Ohio, USA

Figure 8.8.

2. Levin, **Alissa**

b: 20 May 1970
m: Anthony Sebok (divorced)
occ: Graphic designer, founder and principal of Point Five Design
rec: Art, music, dance
currently: New York, New York, USA

Figure 8.9.

3. Levenson, **Judith Sue**

b: 26 Aug. 1958
m: Paul DePesa
occ: Former pre-school director, HeartMath,development assistant
rec: Gardening, hiking, camping, music
currently: Boulder Creek, California, USA

Figure 8.10.

4. Levenson, **Karen Lynn**

b: 18 April 1961
m: Gary Zelcer
occ: Homemaker, health insurance broker
rec: Theater, dance, music, family, friends
currently: Los Angeles, California, USA

Figure 8.11.

* * *

Great-Great-Grandchildren of Sarah Graudan and Julius Isaac Quasser (n=6)

1. Levin, **Isabel Ann**

b: 4 Nov. 2000
rec: Reading, piano, pets
currently: Cleveland, Ohio, USA

Figure 8.12.

2. Levin, **Peter**

b: 8 May 2003
rec: Soccer, baseball, hockey, playing drums
currently: Cleveland, Ohio, USA

Figure 8.13.

3. Sebok, **Max Jacob**

b: 5 Dec. 2005
rec: Geography, piano, dance, and plays
currently: New York, USA

Figure 8.14.

4. DePesa, **Gabrielle Shaina**

b: 15 April 1988
rec: Music, reading, electronics, journaling
currently: Boulder Creek, California, USA

Figure 8.15.

5. Zelcer, **Rachel Leah**

b: 12 June 1993
rec: Reading, writing, poetry, volleyball, piano, swimming, science, theater
occ: Student
currently: Los Angeles, California, USA

Figure 8.16.

6. Zelcer, **Hannah Michelle**

b: 6 Sept. 1995
rec: Piano, music, acting
currently: Los Angeles, California, USA

Figure 8.17.

Robert Herzenberg Memoirs: Life in Libau 1890s to before WWII

Reproduced with kind permission of Robert's Son, Leonardo Herzenberg (www.herzenberg.net).

NOTE: (Editor kwk) Robert Herzenberg was born in September 1885. He was thus about six years younger than my Grandmother Rebecca Holzberg (b. Libau, Oct. 1879) and eleven years older than Jean Michel Linois' Grandmother Henriette Friedlander (b. Libau, Feb. 1896). This description paints a vivid picture of how the Graudans, especially the Founding Siblings, Johanna, Moritz, Rocha, and then later Sarah, and their family would have lived before they spread far and wide to their various fates.

An meinen Sohn (To my son)
LEONHARD HERZENBERG

von (from)

ROBERT HERZENBERG
Memoirs written during the 1940s
Translated during the 1990s by Leonardo (Leonhard) Herzenberg

TRANSLATOR'S PREFACE

I embarked on a translation of this memoir because I wanted to share the information with English-speaking people, and as a way of making myself read it thoroughly, rather than guessing at sections that were not clear. Although we spoke German at home (among other languages), by the time I started this translation I needed a lot of help from a dictionary, and some phrases are still not quite clear. These are quoted in the original German. I use the notation [xxx] to identify page numbers in the original manuscript and (xxx) to indicate page references in the original manuscript. [Ed kwk. To simplify reading I have removed most of the original German words and page numbers.] Most of the section headings appear in the original, but I have added some in natural breaks in the text to make shorter pages.

INTRODUCTION

Oruro, Bolivia.

June 1940

My dear Nardi!

The world war rages and we are for now cut off from all our loved ones in Europe. Who knows when we will again be able to communicate? In a few months you will be six years old and I fifty-three. Who knows whether I will still be there when you are old enough to understand what I want to tell you. And you no longer have any grandparents; from their generation only my uncle Leopold Herzenberg in Libau and few aunts, and on mother's side uncle Edward in Riga and maybe Uncle Jacob. Then mother's aunts Sasha Katz, Lina Shapiro in Riga, Ella Feinberg in Lodz, and Cila Goldstein in Chicago, and an older generation in Latvia. But it is very doubtful that you will ever meet any of them. Hopefully you will have close contact with the younger ones, but they will not be able to tell you anything, since most of them know nothing of the family except for their own close relatives. Thus I will write it all down for you: what I heard from my beloved late father, and what I know otherwise, so that you also get knowledgeable about it and maybe can pass it on. Let's wish that I will still be able to see you mature, and be able to tell you orally what I have summarized here. Otherwise this writing will have to speak for me.

THE REGION

Our origins are in "Kurland" (Latvia). At the time of my birth, and until the end of the (first) World War this was a Russian "Government." Kurland was conquered in the thirteenth century by the German "Orden." The native Letts, who had absorbed the original Kurs, were converted to Christianity. The "Orden" collapsed in 1561. Kurland became a duchy under Polish aristocracy. In 1795 Kurland became part of Russia in the third partition of Poland. The most notable duke was Jacob von Kettler, who was an in-law of the great Elector, who in spite of his dependence on Poland pursued his own policy, had his own fleet, and founded colonies in Guinea and Tobago (Antilles). During the conquest by the German "Orden" Kurland, Livland, and Esthland were Christianized, but by contrast with Prussia, Pommerania, and Mecklenburg, were not Germanized. The landlord spoke only Lettish with his peasants. The pastor preached in Lettish, and there were Lettish schools for the people. The influx of German lasted for centuries. Not only the "Barons,"—i.e., the Aristocracy—who owned the land were German, but everything outside of the peasants was German, such as crafts and commerce. Only the peasant, first as slave, later free, remained Lettish, and subsequently became the industrial worker. Only total Germanization made social upward mobility possible. Therefore the German Baltics slaved away at giving the Letts and Esths the foundations of their culture. They collected their songs and fairy tales, worked on their history and prehistory, worked out the grammar of the languages.

When the Russians started an anti-German policy in the Baltic Sea provinces they found a willing ally in the Letts, who possessed a ready cultural scaffold, forged by the German domination, and knew very well how to use it. In any event, as the Letts, with help from the German Baltic troops, chased away the Soviet Russians, they also drove away the Germans, dispossessed the "Barons," and created their own country of Lettland, where the Letts developed an upper crust for themselves, and more or less forcefully suppressed all other minorities: Germans, Russians, Jews.

At the time of my birth (1885), though, Kurland was still German in its entire culture. The Lett people did not count at all. Kurland came into Russia almost one hundred years after Livland and Esthland, and the energetic Russianization began only under Alexander III. Thus the official language, the administration, the schools, and the high schools were all German. As far as I can remember, everyone in our family spoke high German, with a bit of Baltic sing-song. This was partly reminiscent of East Prussia—e.g., "das Wahser, die Buhter, der Bruhnen." And many local words were used—e.g., "der Herd = die Plite, die Decke = die Oberlage, Eimer = Spann, Sahne = Schmand," etc. But it was a pure German, without Lettish, or Russian loaned words, though once in a while spiced with strong German Jewish wordlets [Wortlein]. As I entered the Libau "Realschule" in 1895, exactly two years had passed since it had been Russianized. Half the teachers now had to teach Russian. They had learned Russian quickly and badly, and taught accordingly.

The pronunciation especially contrasted strongly with that of the Russian teachers. At first we imitated the funny pronunciation, then we spoke that way ourselves; since we only spoke German at home, we were handicapped in Russian. Not only with respect to the pure Russians, who as children of administrators and officers attended the school, but also compared to the Lithuanian Jews who came into the schools from the neighboring [Komnol, Government] and who already spoke Russian at home. But one spoke Lettish with the servants, drivers, and peasants at the market. I still remember distinctly my astonishment when, as a student, I heard Lettish spoken on the "Kornstrasse" in Libau, turned around, and saw three people in wholly European dress speaking the language.

During my youth Kurland still retained its entire uniqueness. The Russianization had only just started. Life was inexpensive. "God's little country" as the Kurlanders called it, was a beautiful and pleasant land. It lies on the Baltic Sea, has many ports, and shipping traffic connects it with the entire world. In the harbor of Libau, sail and steam ships of many lands were anchored. Not just the Baltic neighbors, but very exotic ships would arrive. Before the World War, Libau had a weekly direct connection with North America. The soul of the inhabitants was not narrowly provincial, one had the wide view of the world, representatives of many nations teemed in Libau, and this encouraged stamp-collecting among the students.

MY CHILDHOOD

I was born on 6 September 1885, in Libau, Kurland, in the upper story of the southwest corner of the intersection of Julianen and Ludwig streets. It was 6 Sept., Russian style, where the Julian calendar was still valid. In the Western world one was then twelve days ahead and wrote it as 18 September, but according to the Jewish calendar it was nine Tishri, eve [erev] of Yom Kippur, and as long as my father lived, that day was treated as my birthday. Thus my birthday was never celebrated, since on the eve of the Day of Atonement one had other thoughts in an orthodox Jewish household. One started in the morning with an atonement ritual [kapores-schlagen], in which ones sins are transferred to a sacrificial animal or to money given to the poor. My father had a full-grown rooster, we children copper coins, (the Russian five kopek piece was the size of a [taler]). The copper coins were distributed to the beggars [schnorrergilde], the rooster, however, we consumed in the afternoon before going to the synagogue. Then in the morning a flower pot would be filled with sand in which the meter-long memorial candle for my mother would be placed. So the day already started under gloomy signs, and my birthday was never a happy day.

At my birth my mother got childbed fever. She got through it, but lost her milk and I was raised with a bottle. When we left this house, I do not know. Probably after my mother's death. At that time we lived on the corner of Seestrasse and Schifferstrasse. About 100 meter west of the Seestrasse one came to the beautiful avenue of chestnut trees leading to the spa, and past it directly to the sea. The Schifferstrasse, after about 150 m toward the north, led to the harbor with its warehouses, steamships, and lively activity. There were two apartments on the ground floor, and the same in the next floor. Our apartment consisted of a living room, a bedroom, a dark room, where Aunt Fanny, and later I and cousin Julius, slept, a kitchen, and a tiny garden of about 3 × 3 m. Next to the kitchen was the privy. Libau had sewers later, but no water lines. A W.C would not even be imagined. More of that later. Next to us on the ground-floor lived the carriage owner Abraham Lowenstein. In the courtyard stood his carriages, in the stable the horses. On the upper floor lived a small grain dealer Frank. Behind the fairly large yard there was a neglected fruit garden of the owner Schwerderski. We children would play in the yard and the garden; a ripe berry, pear, or apple would never get into the hand of the owner; we finished everything in the unripe state; it is a wonder that we stayed alive.

Since I was motherless, and the pretty Aunt Fanny was out of the house a lot, I would be left with Lowensteins, or with Frank, and when that did not work with the cobbler Bansemier across the street, with all of whom I spent more time than I did at home. Toys I had none; I played with thread spools and empty boxes. Once a year there was the great annual market in New Libau, and then there might be a wooden horse or some such. Later soldiers were cut out of picture sheets and pasted on cardboard. But I was left to myself, and the whole memory of childhood is very pale. I had measles, scarlet fever, diphtheria, whooping cough—but do not remember any of it. When I was about four, cousin Julius Bernitz, who was two years older, was brought into the house. His father had died, his mother had stayed with the younger children Hemske and Frieda at my grandparents in Goldingen. I grew up together with Julius, and we lived in one room until I left home in 1902. I am conscious of very little of my first years of childhood. I do not know what my age was when my father decided to enroll me in a kindergarten, the only one in Libau, which at that time must have been seen as a daring novelty. Children were raised at home, then went to the cheder, or else the German private school, and from there either in to a yeshiva or into the business.

The awareness of systematic learning in preparation for [university] study occurred only in a later stage of my life, in the '90s. I came into the kindergarten of Miss Rosenpflanzer, an old, white-haired lady, always in a cheerful, happy mood, with rosy cheeks. It was a kindergarten with about twenty children, mostly of Baltic parents; we were only a few Jewish children among them, and naturally no consideration was given to that. Instruction was in a pure Lutheran spirit, and I knew, and sang, several German church songs, to which my father apparently did not object. Emil, the oldest brother of Grinja Falk, was in the same kindergarten, and also later his future wife, Manja Pines, but then she was very young. From there I went into the private school of Ansitt. It was run by two old, haggard, and quite ugly spinsters. There I learned the beginning basics of the Russian language. I was in this school only a short time and came into a further private school of Miss Schafer in the Waisenhausstrasse, a fair stretch to walk, which was not at all nice in winter and in the morning. Aside form Miss Schafer, a broad older and very energetic lady, two Russian ladies, Krefowt and Hubenet, worked there. Instruction was stern and hard; I was not taken seriously, because of my Jewishness, which I did not understand yet.

I only have unpleasant memories of these two private schools, but in the last one my first friendship was made. In class with me there was a blond boy, Kurt Bonitz, the son of the confectionery owner Bonitz. Kurt would invite me over on occasional

Sunday afternoons, there was chocolate, and cake, and ice cream, as much as I could eat. I had a sweet tooth then, and still have it. In exchange I would tell fairy tales. We soon came apart. So ended the year 1894. At that time a preparatory class was added to the Realschule. I was enrolled in it, passed my admission exam, and was dressed in the black uniform that I wore until the summer of 1902. It consisted of black long pants, a military shirt, also black, with an attached black high collar that closed with a hook. Then there was a black patent leather belt with a brass buckle on which black letters were embossed. The initials stand for [Russian words], Libau City Realschule. The cap was black, in military style, with yellow black patent leather visor, and again the initials embossed in the "golden" oak leaf cluster. In winter there was also a coat, black with "gold" buttons. There was another high school in Libau, the humanistic Nicolai gymnasium, named in honor of Czar Nicholas I. At that time in czarist Russia, except for a few military high schools, there were only the two kinds of high schools. Realschulen gave the right to enlist in voluntary military service for a year and then after six years also gave the right to study in the commercial section of the polytechnic university, from which one could graduate in three to four years. Realschulen also had a supplementary class. After graduating from this seventh year, one received the leaving certificate that entitled one to study at polytechnic university, but not at a regular university, unless one also satisfied the requirements of the Greek and Latin curriculum.

Attending the humanistic gymnasium required eight years, where Latin and Greek and a choice of German or French were taught. There was no natural science, and little mathematics and physics. Graduating from the gymnasium opened doors to many universities. They had the same uniforms, but the vizors were white, and the buttons were "silver" instead of "gold," etc., and the winter coat was a light gray. In summer one wore the same style uniform, but made of linen, which was very pleasant in the heat. The great advantage of the uniform was that from the outside there was no indication of difference in wealth between the students in all of Russia. The son of the richest man, while attending school, both in and out of school, wore the same, simple, black clothing as the son of the poorest widow. The girls in the state schools also wore uniforms, though a little room for individuality was left in choice of hair ribbons and lace trimmings. In old Russia everything was uniformed; not only military, navy, police, and customs, but also any government employee wore uniforms, and not only on duty, but also otherwise; and, of course, all school pupils and other students wore uniforms.

Realschulen and gymnasiums were under the ministry of popular education, as well as most universities. However, there were some in the road construction ministry, and others in the mine construction ministry. Later a third kind of higher school was established (known as middle schools in Russia) in the commercial schools. This type of school was modeled after the Realschulen, but had English instead of French, and subjects such as political economy, bookkeeping, etc. The schools had the same rights as the Realschulen, the same black uniforms, but with green vizors since they were under the finance ministry, which also was in charge of its own polytechnic schools, such as those in Warsaw and Kiev, and the mining school in Jekaterinslav (now Dnjepropetrovsk).

When I spoke above of the rights to study that these high schools provided, it was to be understood that applied to all non-Jews. For Jews there was a Numerus Clausus (quota) that limited the number of Jewish students. In Petersburg and Moscow this quota amounted to between 0.5 and 3.0 percent, in the inner lands around 5 percent, and in the rim states and in the settlement districts up to 10 percent.

The quotas were also used in the high schools. Even in the lowest grades there was not always room for every Jewish child that applied. Sometimes the quota was calculated for an individual class, so in a class of seventeen students only a single Jew would be allowed, but in my Realschule the whole school was used, and in the graduating class we were fewer than twenty students, and among them five Jews.

Every Jewish father endeavored to make a university education possible for his sons, since the diploma obtained there gave them residence rights in all of Russia. Jews in Russia were second-class citizens; the quota applied not only to the schools, but for the whole country. The Jew could live where he was born, and other than that in the cities and places where the settlement district to which the Czar province of Poland and a few neighboring governments of the Ukraine and white Russia belonged; but not in the country or the villages. I was born in Libau, and was not allowed to live in Petersburg, Moscow, Kiev, or even Riga. When we went to the country for vacations in summer there were always difficulties with the police. Since they were always poorly paid, and thus easily bribed, usually one could get together. But on the whole it was an unbearable condition. Your grandfather Samuel lived in Moscow for a few years, until finally the expulsion reached him. These conditions lasted into the World War 1914/18. It was grotesque that Jewish soldiers, who were brought to Moscow with wounded transports, were expelled from there. No words from the allied French or English did any good, it was said that one could not change the Jew laws in the critical time of the war, and so these did not fall until the collapse of czarist Russia.

So, to obtain residence rights for all Russia, one had to study in a university, and to do so one had to attend the high school that gave the right to study in a university. In order to get into high school, due to the quota, even young children had to take competitive exams and certification tests. Already as eight- and nine-year-olds we knew that we were Jews, and that because of it we had to suffer and struggle. When Germans, Letts, Poles, or Russians needed only a three to be admitted, among Jewish children with the highest scores, lots would be drawn to determine who was worthy of attending high school. And so it went through university; thus it was not surprising that only the most talented, able, and diligent Jews reached university and in later life accomplished accordingly.

Naturally there was a way of easily overcoming all these difficulties, a magic wand that opened not only high schools and universities, but highest society, the highest government positions, a handful of water: baptism. But the abhorrence of desertion from the faith was so deep that the remedy of baptism was grasped only in the rarest cases, and then only in people with no character who were surely no loss to Judaism. How different from Western Europe where baptism and mixed marriage contributed throughout to the good tone of the Jews. In the east, in spite of repression and persecution, pogroms and lack of rights, even the atheist would never think of repudiating Judaism; in the west the attraction of a lieutenant's uniform was enough. In Russia, when Zionism had not even been thought of, the Jews always considered themselves a people, and were treated as such by the government. One was a Russian subject, but for centuries along with that one was a Jew as one might be a Pole, a Finn, or member of another of the one hundred nations that constituted the Russian empire.

LIBAU, MY NATIVE CITY

Libau, a fishing village in the thirteenth century, became a city in 1625. Libau lies on a 2 km wide tongue of land. West of the city the Baltic Sea spreads out, on the east the Libau Lake, which is 2 to 3 km wide, and 15 km long. In the north of the Libau Lake there is a connection to the Baltic, which is widened by dredging. That is the Libau harbor, about 80 m wide and 6 m deep, protected from the Baltic Sea by breakwaters and seawalls, with only narrow openings for ships. The outer harbor is 8 m deep. The harbor is ice-free almost the entire year, and before the World War it was used by fifteen thousand ships a year. Libau had seventeen consulates, was the biggest emigration harbor of Russia, and had lively industry—linoleum for all of Russia was made in Libau. The castor oil for all of Russia was pressed in Libau, and the herrings for all Russia were imported, sorted, packed, and shipped to Russia. Wood, grain, [and] oil-cake were exported.

Libau was called *Libava* in Russian, *Liepāja* in Lettish. The Russian *lipa* means "linden," and the coat of arms of Libau has a linden on a blue field with a red Kurdish lion leaning against it.

Libau was connected to inner Russia by the Libau-Romnyer railroad. A narrow gauge line connected with Hasenpoth via Grobin. After the World War this line was extended to Goldingen, and a line to Riga was also built, since the old connection ran through Lithuania in places, which had become a foreign country. So the new line was built on Latvian ground.

The city was initially built up only south of the harbor, and spread west almost to the Baltic. In the east the shore of the Libau Lake was swampy and unhealthy, and the burgers did not settle there. In the west the Kurhausalle ended at the Kurhaus, where concerts always took place on summer evenings. The Kurhaus stood at the end of a residential district. A wide outside staircase led to the beach. The Libau beach is the most beautiful beach I have seen in all my travels. The Baltic knows no tides, and except for storms when the waves came up to the Kurhaus, the beach was almost 200 m wide all year, the purest, white, flour-fine sand, no pebbles, no piece of wood. The wide white stripe ran from the seawall until Germany, a marvelous street for wandering. Then the westerly storms would come and cover the beach with waves, which on their retreat would leave a foot-high layer of dark brown seaweed. The latter did not lie long, though; a large part was collected by peasants for fertilizer, and the sand would cover the rest without a trace. The seaweed also brought a lot of amber to the shore, and as children we would collect it eagerly; I had boxes of it, naturally mostly hazel-nut size pieces. To the north the beach ended at the seawall on which one could walk 500 m into the Baltic Sea. 1,500 meters south of the seawall was the men's bathhouse and another 500 m the women's bathhouse. Further south was an open-air swimming pool where anyone could bathe as they liked. The bathing establishments had three classes in each. In the first class one stepped directly into man-deep water, the second was built on the beach and one had to wade for 100 m through shallow water before one got neck deep, and the third one was built further back, so one had to walk through sand for 100 m before getting to the water. In summer one would bathe daily, from mid-June until September, and we children would bathe two to three times a day and romp around in the water for hours. In spite of the fact that I spent a lot of time in the water every summer, I never learned to swim. My father was a good swimmer, but apparently he placed no value on having me learn also; actually I was fearfully kept away from water sports; later, when I was fourteen I was allowed to row, but not to sail. In contrast, your uncle George was an enthusiastic and very able sailor. One would bathe without any bathing suit; when someone wore bathing trunks, there would be whispers of a disorder of his sex parts.

Libau is a marvelous sea-side resort, much better than those on the Riga beach. In summer bathing guests would come from Russia, especially when the Russian court visited the resort for a time. Libauers preferred to spend the summer months in the forested area inside Kurland, but most stayed in the city where they could mind their businesses, and enjoy the resorts, water sport, and the rather good concerts at the Kurhaus. At my time the popularity of Libau as a resort had largely declined. The Baltic idyll was made into a fortress and military harbor. Alexander III had decreed that the main Russian military harbor would be built in Reval. In spite of the freedom from ice, and the good location, he did not want a war harbor in Libau due to the danger of the proximity of the German border. In spite of it the grand dukes persuaded Nicholas II that a war harbor be built in Libau, along with a fortress to protect it. So the construction began feverishly. Directly north of the Kurhaus the large shore battery was erected, which continued until the seawall. There was barbed wire and trenches, which do not suit a modern resort. When my uncle Jacob gave me my first camera, a Pocket Kodak, I went to the shore to snap pictures. I photographed the lighthouse, the pilot tower, the seawall, and so on, and was promptly arrested, led through the whole town, and delivered to the gendarmerie. I was then a pupil in the seventh grade, fifteen years old, and unaware that I had committed a state crime. At that time I was tutoring for the family of the fortress commander, general Petrovich, who spoke up for me and effected the return of the camera, but the roll of film was confiscated, who knows why, since one could buy all the pictures cheaper and better as post cards.

The resort declined, but the city blossomed. In addition to the harbor and commerce activity came the construction of the war harbor and fortress. Officers and engineers with families streamed into Libau. There was a boom in every respect. And that went on till the outbreak of the World War. At that time Libau had a population of one hundred thousand. A strange city, but not an exception in the Russian rim countries. The population consisted of German Balts, Russians, Letts, Jews, and Poles. Added to that the many foreigners, Reich Germans, Danes, Swedes, English, French, etc. Each of these national groups led its own life, had its own associations, festivals, amusements. These circles did not intersect, either socially or culturally, even though they were all loyal subjects of the Czar. The Russians consisted of the government employees, military, police, and navy. Then there were all the lower employees, priests, a few businessmen, entrepreneurs, etc. They clustered around the Russian church in the Waisenhausstrassse; then the garrison church was added. In the war harbor a pompous cathedral was erected, another one was started near the Kurhaus, but was never finished. The Russian "society" was exclusive to uniformed employees, both civil and military. They never learned German, and for them the others did not exist. The German burger, merchants, craftsmen, and factory workers had the trinity church on the main street as a center. It was a beautiful, large church, with what at that time may have been the largest organ in the world, having over ten thousand pipes. I was never in a church in Libau, not even for a church concert. The German Balts enclosed themselves culturally with the equally Lutheran Swedes, Danes, and naturally also the nobility, though few of the "Barons" lived in the town: Vietinghoffs, Behrs, Ostensacken, Borners, who though Lutheran, held themselves apart from the German Balts.

The Jewish community, of about twenty thousand, were also divided into several groups. The main group was the Baltic Jews, with German spoken at home and in the community. Yiddish was understood, but they could not speak it. Hebrew was hardly known. Culturally we belonged to the German middle class, and were closer to the German burger group than to any other national group, and read the "old Libausche Zeitung." This Jewish group would not have survived, however, without the rich Jews from white Russia and Lithuania having automatically joined it. These not only gave the group great capital strength, but they were people with immense Jewish and other knowledge and education. These were the Minsk-Pinskers: Halpern, Luries, Eliasberg, Katsenelsohn, Weisbrehm, and so on. The Kurhausstrasse was an avenue of Jewish villas. One lived well, ate well, but also had an open heart and purse for every artistic activity. No musical or literary greatness or dramatic troop would miss visiting Libau, and at all such occasions the Jews were present in greater numbers than their proportion of the population would have indicated. This Jewish group had the large synagogue across from the local court, the "Choir-schul." Since this synagogue was already so Westernized, the prayer leader, the Chasen of my childhood, Rabinovitsch was accompanied by a boy's and men's choir of ten to twenty voices in four parts. The services were very beautiful, but usually Rabinovitsch sang himself hoarse during rehearsal for the festivals; since the choir could not accompany any other prayer leader, the Choir-schul stayed without Chasen and without Choir. In spite of the choir the synagogue did make an impression of a purely eastern Jewish congregation. Later, though, after I had already emigrated, and my father had become the leader, he made a great effort to introduce the Prussian custom and tradition that the synagogues in Germany had adapted him to. The other Jewish congregation jokingly called itself the "Velvet Schul" [*Sammeter Schul*] (though it has nothing to do with velvet [*sammet*]—this northerly part of Latvia was called [Russian word = *samogitien*] and the inhabitants were *sammeter*); it was located near the east harbor and the Weissenhofstrasse. Its members were the poorest circles of the freshly immigrated, as well as established Latvian Jews, with Yiddish as a mother tongue, real [Golus Juden] who tolerated no Western affinity. They had their own affinity and the two groups came together rarely. The Jewish community was quite self-sufficient. One could go through ones whole life, and except for the government, never have to deal with a non-Jew. There were Jewish servants, carriage drivers, hand workers of every kind, and naturally innumerable businesses, schools (without rights), etc.

The Letts were a group wholly to themselves, with the gothic [Annenkirche] at the hay market. In school there were fewer Letts than Jews, we were good schoolmates but there was no closer contact. Yet another isolated group consisted of Catholic Poles and Lithuanian, who flocked to the Catholic church and the parsonage. But each group lived by themselves, married among themselves, and had their own cemetery. However there was no Lettish cemetery.

The frank was forty kopecs, the crowns fifty-five kopecs, and the dollar two rubles. There was much gold coinage (ten and five ruble), silver coinage (one ruble, a rather large coin, $50k, 25k, 20k, 15k, 10k, and 5k), [and] copper coinage ($3k, 2k, 1k, ½k, ¼k). Naturally one preferred paper money for larger sums, such as travel, since gold was very heavy. And what madman would have doubted the security of paper money. One learned of "drafts" and their collapse, but that had been long ago and could not happen again. One lived in friendship with all neighbors, no one thought of war, or revolution; and yet my generation was to experience so much more war, revolution, state destruction, than hardly any other. But in my youth nobody thought of that, and there were no prophets to predict the uncanny future. Life was beautiful and one had everything. Foods were especially cheap; a full-grown goose cost one ruble, pork was ten kopecs per pound. We had to eat the expensive kosher beef and lamb, which cost eighteen to twenty kopecs per pound; part of the expense was the "Korobka" tax. Fish was available in great quantity; every day one could buy live carp, tench, [and] pike. The ocean shipping brought salmon, flounder (which, thanks to the low salt content in the Baltic sea are a pathetic kind of herring), smelt, and dorschel (a miserable north sea cod-fish). Then there were smoked sprats, herring, flounder, and salmon. In winter only the latter were available, but in summer the market was flooded with the best and cheapest berries and fruit. Strawberries from the garden; blueberries and strawberries from the forest; mushrooms, predominantly chanterells, but also stone yellow boletus and champignons; and apples, pears, nuts, cherries, etc. The time for making preserves came in the fall, and for weeks there was cooking of juices and preserves for the winter, since until early summer there would be nothing fresh except potatoes and beets. Foodstuffs were plentiful and cheap; there also were delicacies from the entire Russian empire, from the White Sea to the Black Sea, from the East Sea to Vladivostok. Never again have I experienced such marvelous fruit, confections, and preserves. Unfortunately we were not allowed to eat caviar, since it came from a non-kosher fish without scales, but in the shops the following kinds were available: [malosol], [payusnaya in fusschen].

Clothing was expensive, since there were no ready-to-wear items. The tailor measured for everything, one bought the cloth and accessories, and so the clothing was made. As long as I was in the parent's home no ready-made shoes were bought either; the shoemaker came to the house, took measurements, and then all supplies needed would be bought from the leather dealer. I knew only rubber boots at that time, no laced ones.

The winters were quite cold; already in the fall one would buy several cords of birch wood. Then one would rent inmates of the prison, who would come into the yard with an overseer, to saw, chop, and stack the wood. The large tile-stoves [kachelofen] would be fired with this in the morning in winter and stay warm for twenty-four hours. Before the beginning of winter all windows were fitted with storm windows, the cracks sealed with paper strips, and a padding layer in which colorful corn-flowers and paper rosettes were placed would cover the window-bench. Only in the spring would the storm windows be put away again. Regarding lighting, I experienced the whole development. First we had quite miserable petroleum lamps, then came the lightning burners. When we moved from Seestrasse 32 to the Tieletz house Badestrasse 32 we got gas lighting, already with glow-mantles. Only shortly before I left home did we get electric lighting.

Libau is not on any river, the water in the Libau Lake is not fit for drinking. Two water tables supplied the city. The first one is only about 10 m deep, but the water is infected. Each house has a pump in the yard. The second water table is about 100 m deep, wonderful, pure drinking water, only a little hard. But only richer house owners could afford such a well. The water rose so high artesially that one could obtain it with a hand pump; later every house had either a wind motor or electric pumps that pumped the water into a tank on the ground floor.

The waste water arrangements were worse, however. There was a sewer system that led waste water into the harbor, but only the fewest modern houses had water toilets. Every house had a waste pit that the toilets emptied into, where all the waste collected. Occasionally a steam pump came by with stink-vessels [stinkfassern] and pumped it all out and dumped it somewhere far out of town. When this work happened, the whole house and neighborhood would be filled with a horrible stench.

MY SCHOOL TIME

In August 1895 I came into the first grade of the Libau State Realschule. It was a large class, with over fifty pupils in three rows of school-benches with two places each. There were place numbers and I was fifty-three or fifty-four, that is either the second worst or third worst pupil. Why? I don't know. I was very distracted, indifferent, careless; at home nobody minded me; mother was ill often, your uncle Erich was a difficult, sickly, child. I did what I wanted, and nobody cared about my schoolwork. When the year ended I was promoted to the second grade, subject to passing three make-up exams, in arithmetic, drawing, and calligraphy. I received tutoring during the summer from a student named Falk, son of the cap maker Falk on the large market, and was promoted. In the second grade (the numbering went up to the seventh, where we would receive the maturity certificate), I was a normal pupil, that is, I was promoted without make-up exams. I was never held back during the whole school time, but by a narrow margin. The best pupils were promoted without exams. The next best only had to pass the written exams, and were excused from the oral ones. I, however, got nothing for free, but always came through. In first grade we had a Russian teacher, A. P. Mossakowoski, a seldom loving, very decent person who went to Riga later and died there shortly before WWII. The math teacher was Friedrich Demme from the Dorpat University, a very able mathematician, a fellow student of Wilhelm Ostwold, both of whom were university assistants at the same time. The latter was also librarian for the quite notable Libau city library in the attic of city hall. Our drawing teacher was Sallos, Leonid Ivanovich, of Greek descent. Not only a good teacher, but also a productive artist. Geography was taught by Dokrenko Muxaure Ubanoburr, a pure administrative soul, who also taught history in higher grades; I can't thank him for any inspiration. He was head of all the classes. German was taught by old Baumgaertel. He had been director of the Realschule; after Russianization he was still tolerated as German teacher. He died soon thereafter, when I was still in the second grade and a German-Russian, Freiberg, with a Napoleon beard became my German teacher. From the second grade on [Russian name] taught Russian. The school inspector was F. Ivan Netchaev. As such he was in charge of all school discipline. He was hump-backed, so his nickname was "hump" [*puckel*]; how cruel children are. No one pitied him, he himself was embittered, strict, and overall not pleasant. He was the nightmare of my schooltime, and remained my Russian teacher until my graduation. As a teacher he was outstanding.

In the third grade we started French with Bastin. We took it for four years, but my success was less than great. Although he spoke French fluently, he was not much of a teacher. What I do know of French I learned by myself in later years. Then we started on algebra, which was also taught by Demme. I again failed totally. Place numbers were not used any more, but I would have been one of the last. But instead of place numbers, a system was introduced in which the smallest and worst behaved, that is the liveliest pupils, were seated in the first row, under the watchful eye of the teacher. There I sat till the end of school, close to the teacher and the board; perhaps that is why I did not discover until later that I was shortsighted; since I traveled around in the world without glasses until 1907, I must have missed many beautiful sights. I was promoted conditionally into the fourth grade, again with three makeup exams, in math, French, and drawing. Actually, if one had three makeup exams one was kept back, but drawing did not count as a full subject. This time my tutor was again Falk, and I was promoted. After that I had no further makeup exams. From the fourth to the sixth grade I was an average pupil; in the last two years I was a good pupil, but I was never one of the best, the pride of the class, because I was always lacking in the most important subject: Russian. Although I had contact and friendships with 100 percent Russian schoolmates, in the home, in the family, and in the city one spoke mostly German, and Russian was the foreign language. In August 1899 I came into the fifth grade, during which I became fourteen years old, and my learning started to have sense and purpose. In fifth grade we started with chemistry and mineralogy as natural science subjects, after we had started with biology and zoology and botany in the earlier grades. As teachers we had first (Jagodowski) and later (Roshdestwenski, like the Russian admiral in the battle of Tsusima). Both were Russian intellectuals, but neither was a model of either teaching skill or character. I was very friendly with both of them. They had studied natural science, but had hardly any knowledge of the chemistry and mineralogy they had to teach. And there my schoolwork finally got sense and direction. I built all the apparatus for demonstration of chemical experiments, and made all the experiments, since the teacher had two left hands. These experiments I also had to demonstrate at the girl's gymnasium, and wherever Roshdestwnski gave chemistry lectures. I got practice in glass blowing and experimenting that would later be very handy. The school also had a small mineral collection that nobody took care of. I organized it as well as I could. I was excited and eager, what nonsense I did there; since no one gave me any direction, I pasted together a collection of crystal models, among which I still remember a marvelous pyramid-octahedron with in-going angles. No one was there to tell me that such a thing could not exist in nature; that the axis sections 1:1:n, even with n = infinity, could give a rhombus-dodecahedron only in the limiting case. However, my miss-form was unhesitatingly and admiringly pointed out in the collection.

In any case, from fifth grade on it was clear to me that I would study at university level, that I would study chemistry, and since universities were closed to Realschule students, I would study [to be a] chemical engineer at a "polytechnic" (as the Russian technical universities were called). I had no idea at that time of what a tangled thread my studies would follow, that I would, indeed, study chemistry, that I would become an engineer, that my study and occupation would finally peak on chemical mineralogy. More of that later. I was promoted to the sixth grade after the usual examinations, [and] then took the maturity exam—that gave one the right to volunteer for service in the army for a year. Then I went into the seventh, or completion, grade; with graduation, I had the right to attend a technical university, with the constraint of the quota. I was no longer the bratty rascal of earlier times, but still rather childish. In all classes I was the second youngest; only a Russian schoolmate was a few months younger. I passed my exams well, though not with brilliance, but still with the hope of university study. I carried on with chemistry at home through self-study. The room in which I and cousin Julius slept was my realm. Occasionally something would explode, or I would stink up the whole house. I had a lively interest in pyrotechnic, made "Bengal Matches" (matches that burn with a colored flame) and similar things; I still wonder that I did not fly up into the air along with the whole house with the abundance of mixtures of potassium chlorate that I handled. But this was no longer part of the school requirement; neither was my activity with astronomy. I studied the star charts diligently, and am still rather familiar with the starry sky, though I am less current with the southern sky (which I was not used to). My pride was that I turned to Camille Flamarion and applied for membership in the Societe Astronomique de France, and he answered in a friendly way and I became a member. I received the yellow journal every month. I felt my membership and felt great. Even in later years I would observe the stars whenever I could. With school subjects it was different. In mathematics and physics, which the school director Dobrosrakov taught (a wonderfully good person with a weakness for the soul catching (evangelism) for the Russian Orthodox church, in whose house I spent much time), I was above average. I was always in a struggle with the Russian language; school compositions were always a horror for me. In drawing I was always weak, and though I had a great longing to be able to draw well, it did not work. While many schoolmates were doing figure drawing, and some were working with clay, I kept bungling with ornaments. In contrast I was so much the better in singing class; unfortunately my good memory let me sing faultlessly by ear, and so I never learned to read notes, since that was not actually taught.

Sport was hardly known then. I also had no interest in it; I have never attended a football game or anything similar. In school there was gym instruction, for which we were led to the city gym next to the old German theater on the Herrenstrasse. I was already rather corpulent during my school time, and had exceptionally weak arm muscles, so I was good for nothing. I could not do the simplest thing on any apparatus, and also never learned to climb. I was the shame of Knigge, the gym teacher. When I learned to ride a bicycle skillfully he got reconciled with me. So there was little bodily activity for me: rowing and bicycling. In winter even these disappeared, and I never could learn to skate. No other ice sport was known then. The gymnasts leased the swan pond each year, which became a great skating rink in winter. We Realschule pupils made a competing rink, but it was always a deficit enterprise; I was steward, but as soon as I put on skates I'd be sitting on the ice. I stood out from my age mates, I was no gymnast, no skater, no dancer; always very busy, I also did not participate in afternoon walking around and flirting on the Kornstrasse and the Kurhausprospect; In the world of girls, I was never even noticed, and in the family people shook their wise heads thoughtfully about this strange boy who made powders, swallowed stars, did not care for any girlfriend, and busied himself with the strangest things.

During the last school years, when I was in the fifth to seventh grades, I had every Sunday afternoon set aside. At that time there was in Libau a Commission for Popular Lectures. Every Sunday afternoon there were popular lectures on science, literature, and occasionally Russian holy legends, illustrated with slides. I was the projectionist, so I had to set up the projector, set up the screen—since the slides were projected from the stage—and after the lecture put everything away, all without compensation. When I left the school I received certificate of thanks, with a silver [Teton?] as memento. Naturally I was considered an expert for slide projection, and whenever a slide lecture took place, whether it was in the war harbor to fight alcoholism among the sailors, or in the imperial technical association, the projector and I were a permanent fixture. Those Sunday afternoons, and the Saturday afternoons also, were occupied with such useful activity. Libau had a rather nice city library, located in the attic of city hall. Mostly there was old German trash that no one took care of, but there was also a modern section with literature, travelogues, etc., which were loaned out quite a lot. The city librarian was my math teacher Demme, and he entrusted me with loaning out books; so every Saturday afternoon I sat there loaning out and taking back books, and was lost to family life that mostly took place at that time. This must have been sad for my parents, but I was already known as an odd one.

During my school time my education in two other subjects ended for me: music and religion. When I was in the second grade in 1896 it was decided that I should take violin instruction. During my childhood, when I listened to the concerts in the Kurhaus garden almost daily during the summer and was acquainted with almost all the musicians, I showed strong interest. Then, after my father's second marriage, the concert visits stopped. In school I sang in the choir until my voice changed, always in the first voice, but did not know a single note, because due to my good memory I sang everything correctly with ease. Now I was to learn music. In Libau there was a city orchestra, with about a dozen old musicians. The violinist Weissborn also taught, and I wanted to learn with him. Maybe I would have learned violin in spite of my short, thick fingers, but the family council decided it differently. Around that time a Berliner, Hand Hochapfel, and his wife came to Libau and opened a music school. There I was stuck in spite of my protests. He was a very good violinist, pianist, and conductor, but had no talent as a teacher, no patience, and I felt very unhappy with him. There were three students in the one-hour lesson. Each one played for ten minutes and waited twenty minutes to have another turn. That amounted to two times ten minutes per hour. The progress = zero. I learned the first position, the third position, which took several years; in the sixth grade the high pressure of final exams was present. I had to abandon all extra-curricular activities, so the music lessons were dropped, though I don't think I would ever have learned much with that system.

Religion instruction ended even earlier, that is, working with the teacher [Melamed]. With the deeply religious stance of the parents it was natural that much weight would be given to religious education. But no Jewish teacher came to the house, as happened later with my brothers Erich and George. Instead, I went to the cheder on Sunday and holiday afternoons and during school vacations. The cheider was led by Melamed Ilja Blumenau, a bankrupt merchant, who was married but had no children, or they had left home, since they were never mentioned. All ages were in a single room, the bigger boys in front, the younger ones in the back benches, where the helper chait supervised.

Blumenau was a quite good teacher, spoke a pure German, and a pretty good Russian, but that did not matter, since the main thing for a Melamed was to be strict, and Blumenau trained the children in an unbelievable way. While in the Russian Realschule beating was absolutely forbidden, where in the time from the preparatory classes to graduation I never received a single stroke or pinch, where even the smallest pupil was addressed formally, but the teachers, in the Russian way, were never addressed with family names or titles, but only with given name and father's name, Blumenau's students were beaten from early till late. Every small error resulted in ear slaps, and near the desk stood and hung a large selection of canes and leather straps with which he worked over the boys according to mood and severity of error. It always hurt, and much, but neither me nor other pupils souls were damaged by it. I learned to read Hebrew quickly and confidently, and some translation, which only was considered for the main parts of the Jewish bible [Tanach]. One had to be able to read the prayers without error, but translating them was something even my father could not do. At home we prayed the morning prayer, in the evening the [Krischma}, and at meals the table prayer. A little Hebrew grammar was done, which was hopelessly pointless, since for a true Melamed any grammar was a laughable Western invention. The most trouble was the [Raschrift] and the [Schulchan-Oruch], the most pleasure for me was the [tropp], the sing-song with which the Torah and Haftorah were recited. Then my bar mitzva came along. I had Parsche and Haftora and spouted everything, then I gave a speech at home that Blumenau had copied somewhere and I had to memorize. Everyone was touched, I less so, but I was happy about the more than one hundred books I got as gifts. After the bar mitzva I went to Blumenau for another year; he was to teach me the elementary foundations of the Talmud. He started with the Baba metzia, but it did not go, it definitely did not go. Then Blumenau, who believed in natural remedies, got sick and treated himself with liquor and about six other methods. When he clearly did not improve he let a doctor see him, who was no longer able to help him, he cured himself to death.

And with that my Jewish education ended. Until I left home I prayed every morning with Tefilim. I kept getting more hostile to religion, but dared not do anything against my father's convictions. What I know of Hebrew I learned later exclusively from self-study; I copied and translated the entire Tanach, still in the year 1932. I have not prayed since I left home, and have not fasted, but always had deep respect for all Jewish religious activity, from concern with my ancestors and all Jews for whom it is still sacred today.

Sarah Quasser's (b. Graudan) Diary: Return Trip to Latvia, July 1928

Reproduced with kind permission of Sarah's Granddaughter Ruth Kalin.

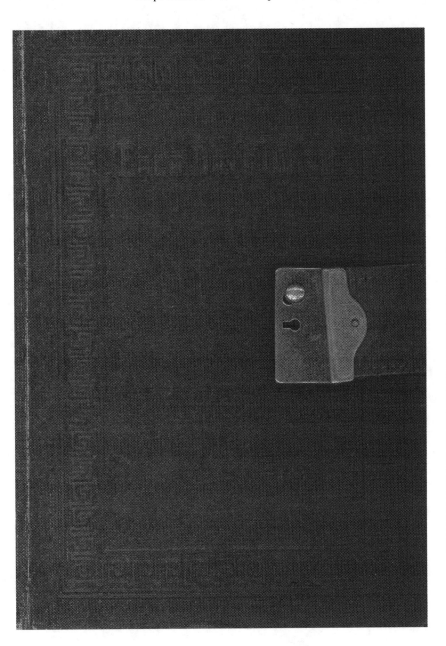

Family Mentioned in Diary

Sarah Quasser (born Graudan and married to Isaac), traveled with her daughter Judith. They visited Sarah's sister Rahlehen (Rocha Friedlander, born Graudan) and her middle daughter Jenny. Fimy was almost certainly the nickname for Rocha's eldest daughter Dina who was married to Walodia.

Sarah went to visit the grave of her brother, Moritz. Flora was Moritz's wife. Colya (Nicholas Graudan) and Lussia were the children of Moritz and Flora. Fanny was Isaac Quasser's sister.

The others were all friends.

Figure A2.1. Trip to Europe with Daughter Judith, 1928

JUNE 1

I have decided to accompany
1928 Judith on her "Great Tour
Trip to Europe" which she won
in the contest of the Morning Sun
on May 19 - 1928.

19 The contest lasted for 8 weeks
after hard work Judith was victorious
having 11,500000 votes, twice as much
as the two other winners. Hurrah.

19 All our friends and Judith pupils
were very loyal towards her. It made
us feel proud and happy to know the
great interest they have shown in her

19 As soon Judith won her trip
she begun to ask me and I feel
that I should go with her - I could
not think as a possibility and

19 laughed at her - Judith was
willing to change the date of her departure, instead of July 4 for June 13 which
gave us only 11 days to prepare for
our trip. How excited I am. —

Figure A2.2. Page 1, June 1, 1928

148

JUNE 1

I have decided to accompany Judith on her Great Tour Trip to Europe, which she won in the contest of the Morning Sun. on May 19, 1928. The contest lasted for eight weeks. After hard work Judith was victorious having 11,500,000 votes, twice as much as the two other winners—Hurrah. All our friends and Judith's pupils were very loyal toward her. It made us feel proud and happy to know the great interest they have shown in her. As soon as Judith won her trip she began to ask me and Dad if I should go with her. I could not think as a possibility and laughed at her. Judith was willing to change the date of her departure time, instead of July 4 for June 13, which gave us only ten days to prepare for our trip. How excited I am.

JUNE 2

The first step toward our trip was to go to the Court House to apply for a passport. I went downtown at 10a.m., and shopped until late in the afternoon. Dad bought me a fine suitcase as a present and paid $18 for it, and then we both selected presents for five graduants. Dad and I had luncheon at Hurth's Café shop (Judith went to a Bridge Luncheon at Mathews; announcement of Lilian's engagement). I have accomplished more than I expected. I found a pair of shoes, a hat, some underwear, and two dresses. So I am fixed up for my trip, except sending clothes to the cleaner. I have more work to do to bring everything in order, than to prepare for the trip, as I do little preparation for it.

Skip To . . .

JULY 10

The train to Semgallen was too occupied; we could not get a sleeper. We were sitting up and talking with Raissa. Poor soul, she is very unhappy and is taking the death of her mother very hard. Two stations before Semgallen Raissa left us. We found other travelers with whom we traveled till Riga. We arrived there at 5p.m. Guttman Rose was at the depot and took us to the Hotel Metropole. He was sorry that his family is living at the seashore and could not entertain us in his home. We were very tired but had no time for a rest, as we wanted to see Chaizen. I knew she will start to lament that we did not stop at her house; believe me, she did enough, but she could not persuade us to move to her house. This time we were more than smart not to do it. We would have been dead to hear all her complaints.

JULY 11

Everyone was so glad to see us and showed us friendship and love. Guttman was lovely to us. He made all arrangements, called up Rose Maditus, asked her to call up the whole family Kahn; also Uncle Kahn's daughter, Anna, to meet us at the Wehrmanschen Park. There was some excitement as everyone of our relatives expected to meet us at the depot with flowers and a brass band. They could not forgive us to have them all dissapointed. We stayed one day in Riga. We were at Chaizen for dinner, at Meditus for supper, at Mary Kahn for breakfast, at Z. Kahn for luncheon, and these Guttmans took us the next day to his summer house where we had dinner at Hermans. We had supper where we met their sister Rose. Also Marcus Kahn with his wife. It was very interesting to see all relatives with their families.

JULY 12

At 10p.m., we left Bilderingshof in Riga. All our relatives were at the depot to bid us goodbye. We were sorry to leave them so soon. We were glad we became a sleeper from Riga to Libau where we had rest. I woke up early in the morning and could not go to sleep anymore for excitement. Finally, the conductor called Leipaja. There we were. I recognized everyone, but it seemed to me they have all changed. The young ones became grown up. The grown-up became old. I found Rahlehen and Samuel, gray and very aged. Flora is better preserved than the other ones. Colya, Lussia, and Jenny had changed. Have no words to describe the joy of seeing them all again. It seemed like a pleasant dream to us. Fanny, Max, Lony, Fimy, Walodia, Flora, Colya, Lussia, Rahlehen, Samuel, Jenny, all were at the depot. We went home with Rahlechen. We all ate the wonderful *kugel*. We had an *Etrogstorte,* and the house was like a flower garden.

JULY 13

Now again, all the questions about everyone and everything! I answered how much I could. We had a lovely dinner at Rahlehen. We went to the Tbra for supper. I do not need to say what I felt when we came to Flora, but we both were very brave. Colya and Lussia played for us. It is a *Hochgenuss* to hear them play. Rahlehen gave me a letter from Paris, which she received for me from the *Art Knaft Bureau.* We asked them if they could extend our trip for one week. They accepted it and wrote us to return to Cologne July 28. This was an enormous joy for all of us.

JULY 14

Although we have in Libau terrible cold weather, nevertheless I started to take cold bathe in the Baltic Sea. It is a pity how quiet it is on the Strand. It seems everyone is waiting for warmer weather. I persuaded Lussia and Colya to go in swimming with us. How much I am enjoying a swim in the old Baltic Sea! I am wearing my winter coat daily and believe me, I am not too warm. I think Libau is further than the North Pole. It seems the sun is colder there and the winds are so icy, it goes through you. They say they never have such a cold summer. I suppose the weatherman wants to teach us with a cold summer for all the heat we had in USA.

JULY 15

We have Sunday today. Rahlehen has Colya and Lussia for dinner as Flora went out of town. Judith and I went first for a good swim, then we will enjoy better our good dinner. Helena Leibowitz came to see us and brought flowers. Some other friends brought candy. Everyone seems to be happy that we are with them, but think I have not changed much and look well Fimy and Walodia took Judith for a buggy ride. We will all meet at Fimy's house for supper. I think Fimy is looking fine and happy with her husband. He is a very fine man. Sorry they have such a cold season. It was very unfavorable for Walodia's business.

JULY 16

Flora and I went to the cemetery this morning. What I felt to see the grave of my dear brother Moritz, of my parents, and of so many old friends of whom I did not know they were dead. I was horrified to know how many died in this fourteen years. I did not tell Judith where we were going. I did not want for her to have such traumatic impressions. I met the children at the *Badehaus* later on and went for dinner at Flora where we stayed also for supper. Rahlehen, Fimy, and the others came to Flora and we spent a nice evening among ourselves.

JULY 17

The routine of today was the same. We went swimming. Had dinner and supper at Fanny. Fimy and Jenny were with us. I stayed with Fanny the whole afternoon. Flora and Lussia came there for tea. I had to write many letters (as usually). In the evening, I went to the Samiter synagogue where a wonder boy, Jossele Maizel, eleven-year-old, sang in a choir. I was surprised that this old synagogue, of which my father, Israel, was the founder and president for many years, was kept up so nicely. It had even many modern improvements—electric lights, better ventilations. We all went, even Lussia, Colya, and Jenny, and all enjoyed their chanting. Judith did not like that the women sat upstairs.

JULY 18

It seems we are so busy with doing nothing that we even were not yet at the "Kurhaus" to a concert, so we have decided to do it tonight. A lady singer is going to give a concert accompanied by a pianist. It was pretty fair. After the concert, we all went to Moritz Coffee at the Kaiser Pavilion, where they had a few entertaining numbers—violins, singing. We liked best a new Russian song (Bubletzky). Jimy gave the song to Judith. We will see if our American friends will like it. Today was Rahlehen's day to have us for dinner and supper. To satisfy everyone, we are eating one day at Rahlehen, second day at Flora, third day at Fanny. We are eating —Teg. Hope nobody will ask us to eat on Yom Kippur.

JULY 19

Was the day we had to leave Libau to return to Cologne on July 21. We are all glad that we have the permission to stay here one week longer. We were at Fanny for dinner today. After dinner, Fanny and I went to call on Mrs. Westerman (Baskind). She was not feeling well and could not come to see us, but she had sent a beautiful plant. They entertained us lavishly. Everyone was asking about everybody. Poor me! I had to talk some more with my sore throat. We went over to see Helena Leibowitz, also her son Adolph from Berlin is visiting them. He is a nice fellow. We had supper at Rahlehen and we played casino with Uncle Samuel. I was too tired to go to the Kurhaus.

JULY 20

Being so busy, I intended to write several letters, which I had neglected to do it, especially to Riga to thank them all for their hospitality. All at once Anna Alperiowitz came in. As soon as I saw her, I knew some excitement was in store for me. So it was. Rosengarden promised to lend some money to her, Anna's husband, but he did not have any. They wanted I should give a certain amount of money. Then they, H. and I. Gutman, will give the same amount. I figured and figured I hated to do it without Isaac knowing it, but Alperiowitz's were in such bad circumstances, I had to do it. Hope Isaac will understand and not be angry with me. We had supper with Fimy in the evening. I stayed home with Samuel and Rahlehen. Judith, Jenny, and Lussia went to a Kino. We are calling it movie.

JULY 21

This was the busiest day. I cannot see how we did it to be at all these places. We had breakfast at Rahlehen, went bathing at 12, had dinner at 3p.m. with Fanny, at 4 we went to Judelson (Schachmowitz). I promised her to take her daughter with us to Berlin. From 6 to 8, we went to Paula Sonnen . . . she had Emma S. Friedman and Zilla Gerson with her (Lieverman), both old friends of mine. Was glad to see them all. They asked us all to visit them, but had to refuse. From 8 to 10, we went to supper to Leibowitz (for supper) and from there, we went with Graudans and Jenny to the new opened Bonitz Conditorei, where the youth was dancing. We returned at 2.

JULY 22

Another Sunday in Libau and the last one. So our dear ones decided to take an excursion for Bernathen, 14 Europe miles from Libau. Lussia and Colya went on their bicycles. Walodia, Fimy, Fanny, Lony, Jenny, Judith, Chaizin, and daughter went on a big horse and wagon. Rahlehen, Flora, and myself went on a bus, which goes every few hours from Libau by to Bernathen. The Gersons found this road in Bernathen (where there) is a full roadhouse where you can get hot and cold drinks. Fanny, Flora, and Rahlehen furnished the food. Judith and I the drinks and we enjoyed ourselves immensely. Lussia, Colya, Judith, and Jenny even went swimming. For change, we had a lovely, friendly day. Chaizin and her daughter are spending here a week with Fanny Hurwitz.

JULY 23

Every day draws nearer to our departure. I really hate to leave Rahlehen; therefore, I am having (the last) dinner with her at 6 o'clock. We promised to visit Abramowitzes. Judith is still remembering *geschmerte matzos*, which she ate about eighteen years ago. So she is fixing again this wonderful dish for Judith. Rahlehen, Fanny, and Helena were with us there also. We had a regular spread, stayed there till 8:30, and from there Rahlehen, Jenny, Judith, and I went to the Stadt Theater. Flora and Colya brought the tickets for us all to see a Jewish singer and impersonator. It was very good. I was surprised to see a full house. It seems though that everyone is too poor to go to theater.

TUESDAY, JULY 24

After having a nice cold swim (I went by myself as it was so cold and unfriendly), I went to Flora for dinner. Judith, Colya, and Lussia did not go bathing. I found Judith there. Flora made me lie down and then we all went to Goldman's for tea. Mrs. Goldman insisted having us for supper, but we refused, as we wanted to be at Flora and hear Colya and Lussia play. Mrs. Goldman had, as everyone else, a wonderful spread. Had her sister, Frau Rathaus, Fran Ettinger, Frau Ginzberg over (old friends of mine). We spent a lovely afternoon. In the evening, Fanny and Walodia came over to Flora and we had the pleasure of hearing Coyla and Lussia give a fine concert. How I wish they would come to America.

WEDNESDAY, JULY 25

I got up early this morning to start to do my beloved job in packing. I was through by 1 o'clock. Went by myself bathing. Judith preferred to stay home and do some shopping afterwards. Went to Fanny for dinner, did some shopping in the afternoon. When I returned, I found many friends of mine waiting for me. Helena Leibowitz, Helene Nevrasky, and Henrietta Salkin, an old schoolmate of mine. They all felt badly that we are leaving tomorrow—flowers, candy, and presents as usually. Everyone is lovely to us. Fanny and Flora with their families came over after supper to Rahlehen and stayed till midnight. We were so tired that we had to go to bed to rest up for tomorrow. How I hate to bid them goodbye.

THURSDAY, JULY 26

Abscieds morgen. I heard Rahlehen getting up so early. Poor soul. I know how badly she is feeling. I got up also to be with her a few more hours. Helped her fixing our lunch. Our direct train to Berlin has no dinner till late in the evening. I tried to cheer her up. Samuel had to go to his business place, so we bade him goodbye at home. For a long time, I will not forget *diesen abschied* and the words he spoke. All relations, friends, acquaintances were at the depot. Lony took some pictures of us before our departure. When I kissed Rahlehen goodbye, I thought I'm breaking down and don't know if we will see each other again. Hope to the Lord he will spare their lives for a long time. We were glad that Colya was with us.

152

FRIDAY, JULY 27

One incident when we reached Lithuania, the officer took our passport and found out that our transit visa were two days overdue. We had to get a new visa, but did not have any money but dollars, which they did not accept. Luckily Colya had Lithuanian Litas. He saved the day for us. We are calling him Dollar Nephew. After having a nice trip first class from Libau to Berlin and then Berlin to Cologne in a very comfortable train and had a sleeper, we arrived in Berlin 9a.m.

Skip To . . .

COLUMBUS: Sunday AUGUST 26

We were all happy to see each other after eleven weeks. I telephoned right away to Isaac and he came to Columbus on Sunday noon. Now, I had to tell them all about Europe, our trip, and especially about all the relatives. I brought for all little remembrances, also some presents for Anna from her sisters. I was so glad that Marcus was feeling better again. Hope he will stay well now. We left Columbus 6:30 and arrived in Portsmouth 9:30. Adolph and May were waiting for us. I found the house nice and clean. Isaac had a big cake (written "Welcome Home" on it) and nice flowers on the table and the table set for supper. It was very attentive of him to do it.

PORTSMOUTH: MONDAY, AUGUST 27

It is nice to travel, but it is nice to come home again. I did some unpacking today. Isaac insisted I should not cook today, and we went to Hurth's for dinner as his guest. In the evening, many of our friends came to see me and all thought I was looking fine and that my bobbed hair was becoming to me. I never wrote home that I had bobbed my hair in Lodz. This was a surprise for them. Isaac did not care at all. I bought presents for all the ladies who were so lovely to remember us before we left for Europe.

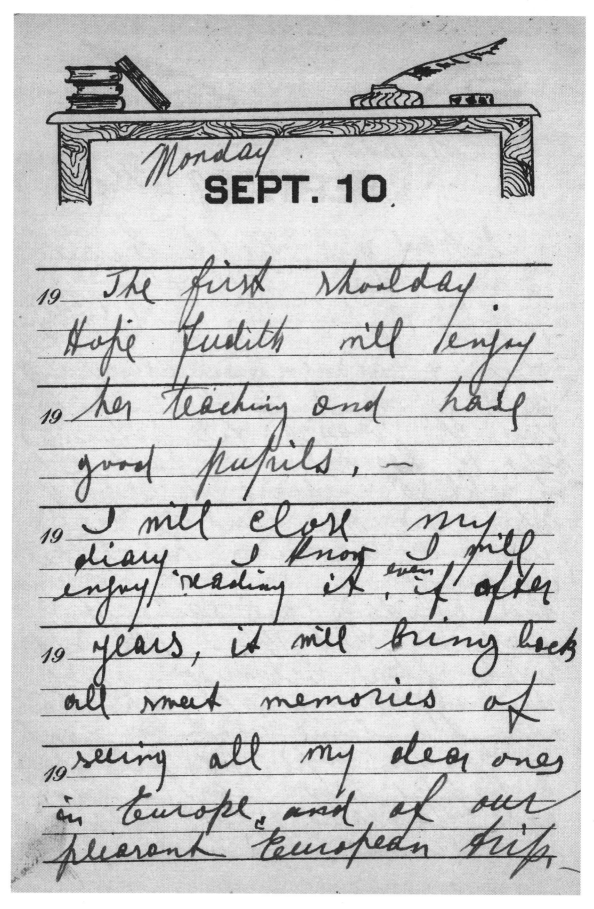

Monday

SEPT. 10.

19 — The first schoolday
Hope Judith will enjoy
19 — her teaching and have
good pupils, —
19 — I will close my
diary I know I will
enjoy reading it, even if after
19 — years, it will bring back
all sweet memories of
19 — seeing all my dear ones
in Europe, and of our
pleasant European trip

Figure A2.3. Last Entry

Reproduced from *Jews in Liepāja, Latvia. 1941–45: A Memorial Book*, by Edward Anders and Juris Dubrovskis (Burlingham, California: Anders Press, 2001). With kind permission of the Authors.

NOTE: (Editor kwk) We do not know for sure where, or exactly when, Rocha and Jenny died. We do know they were still alive in August 1941. This haunting description, by a survivor, describes what some of our family suffered. It may well be that Rocha was murdered at Šķēde and possibly Jenny survived a while longer to live in the Liepāja Ghetto.

THE TRAGIC FATE OF LIEPĀJA JEWS[1]

Solomon Feigerson

These reminiscences of the tragedy of Liepāja Jews are an indictment, exposing the crimes of the Nazi executioners and the grief and suffering of innocent people who were murdered or crammed into a ghetto and jailed in concentration camps.

Dedicated to my grandsons, Daniel and Tom

LIEPĀJA IN 1941

Liepāja, a small Latvian town on the Baltic Sea coast, was famed for its wonderful beaches and old parks. It had an ice-free commercial port, as well as the navy base Kara osta (German: Kriegshafen), north of the town.

Before World War II, the Jewish population of Liepāja numbered about 7,400, out of a total of 57,000. The life of the Jewish community was diverse and intensive, thanks to the activities of various organizations and parties, such as *Agudat Yisroel, Trumpeldor, Hashomer Hatsair*, and others. Children between the ages of six and sixteen attended Jewish or Latvian schools. There was a Yiddish gymnasium, as well as Jewish evening schools and trade schools. About ten synagogues existed in the town.

When Germany attacked the USSR on 22 June 1941, the Soviet army and navy garrison, supported by "Workers' Militia" volunteers (among them many young Liepāja Jews), defended the town against the enemy onslaught for seven days. The fighting was fierce. Raids by dive bombers escalated daily, and after heavy bombardment by naval and land-based artillery during the night of 28/29 June, German troops seized the town. There was much damage to the center of town, and only two synagogues remained intact: Beis Midrash and the Choral Synagogue, both on Kuršu street.

An *SS-Einsatzgruppen* team arrived on the heels of the soldiers, and began executions of Jews. Not to be outdone, the army and navy joined in the persecutions. On 5 July, a week after occupation of the town, the newly appointed commandant, Korvetten-Kapitän Brückner, issued a set of draconian rules for Jews.

1. All Jews must wear a bright yellow marker (at least 10 ×10 cm) on their chests and backs.
2. All men between the ages of sixteen and sixty must assemble in the Firehouse Square at 7a.m. every day for public works. *(Mostly they were brought to the navy base, on open platforms attached to the streetcars. These were jam-packed with Jews in both winter and summer.)*
3. Jews must observe a curfew, being allowed to leave their homes only 10–12 and 15–17.
4. Jews must surrender all means of transportation, weapons, uniforms, radios, and typewriters.
5. Jews are forbidden to: (a) change their place of residence, (b) use sidewalks, (c) use public transportation, (d) enter parks, cinemas, libraries, (e) attend schools.

Food was rationed for all civilians, but Jews got much smaller rations than others and were allowed to shop only at one

---

1   Translated from Russian by Helena Belova, edited by Edward Anders.

special store. There usually was a long queue, and many people left empty-handed, as the store ran out of goods or the curfew hour approached. Sometimes we went hungry for several days.

Right after the seizure of Liepāja, the SD established itself at Kūrmājas avenue 21. That building acquired a sinister reputation, as people were tortured there. The chief, SS-Untersturmführer (lieutenant) Wolfgang Kügler, was assisted by Oberscharführer Carl-Emil Strott and Scharführers Handke, Holer, Schweig, Baumgartner, Reiche, Kaiser, Krapp, Sobeck, Michalsky, and others. Their main activity was systematic murder of Jews.

Naturally, the two synagogues in Kuršu street that had survived the assault of the town also had to be destroyed. The Nazis did not venture either to blow them up or to burn them, as they were located among numerous wooden houses. Instead, they forced Jews to demolish the synagogues. They drove Jews together in Kuršu street, who then pulled down the wooden synagogue Beis Midrash under supervision of policemen. Local people "salvaged" planks and logs. The Choral Synagogue, being built of stone, was a tougher task, requiring crowbars. In keeping with the spirit of the times, Jews from all walks of life were forced to do the job: dressmakers and physicians, cobblers and lawyers, all pressed into a wrecking crew. For the Nazis they were all the same: Jews. While demolishing the Choral synagogue, one man fell from the wall to his death. The others had to wait a few months for their turn to come.

After the synagogues had been demolished, the SD carried the humiliation a step further. They unrolled the sacred scrolls on the Firehouse Square, and SS-Untersturmführer Kügler rode over them on horseback. The Jews, herded together from all parts of town, had to watch the Nazis desecrating their Torah.

There had been repeated mass arrests and executions of several dozen Jews at a time since the beginning of the occupation, carried out by firing squads of the SD and German police, with some help from the army and navy (who in any case furnished large numbers of spectators[2]). But apparently the pace was not fast enough, as the Arājs Commando, a team of Latvian volunteer killers, arrived from Rīga on 21 July in their notorious blue buses, and shot more than six hundred Jews in a three-day orgy of murder. Jews—mainly men over sixteen but also some women and younger boys—were seized in the streets or apartments and then driven, with their hands up, to the execution site: the pre-1914 casemates near the lighthouse. Any resistance was punished by severe beatings. During that round-up, my father Yakov Feigerson was arrested and killed.

The arrests, though directed by German officials from the SS, Gestapo, and SD, were carried out by Latvian "self-defense" men (later renamed auxiliary police or *schutzmänner*). I must point out that all the Latvian Schutzmänner who took part in the roundups (and later, executions) were volunteers. It was hard to believe that former friends had turned into heartless enemies, that some neighbors, who had been living next door for years, were waiting for the moment when the Jews would be arrested in order to loot their home. Many who had the opportunity hastened to make a fortune out of Jewish blood. They snatched as much as they could; Jews were outlaws. We were proclaimed to be a criminal race deserving complete extermination.

A major factor was the relentlessly vicious anti-semitic propaganda, which blamed the Jews for everything. Allegedly it was the Jews who had run the hated Soviet government, especially the NKVD that had deported, tortured, and killed people. It was the Jews, not German bombs and shells, that had burned down much of the town center. (Inconveniently, some of the most heavily burned-out streets, such as Vītolu iela, had many Jewish resident, but a German police document[3] nicely rationalized this seeming paradox: the Jews had burned down their own houses out of spite, to deny them to the Germans.) The *Protocols of the Wise Men of Zion* were serialized in the daily paper, which also offered an explanation for occasional disappearances of children in past decades: the Jews had used their blood for matzos! Served this daily barrage of lies, people with stunted intellect or ethics could easily find rationalizations for murder, theft, or at least indifference.

The arrests and murders were nearly continuous. The Nazis hastened to eradicate the spirit of Judaism in this part of Hitler's empire, shooting well-known artists, scholars, athletes, etc. Among them were the composer and director of the local theater Walter Kahn, physician Aaron Schwab, choirmaster of the Choral synagogue Rabinovich, gabbai Joffe, and athlete Heske Levinstein.

I shall discuss Heske separately. His nemesis was the well-known Liepāja boxer Holcmanis, who had become a

---

2   Landgericht Hannover: *Strafurteil gegen Grauel und andere (2 Ks 3/68 30/28a 5/68)*, 1971.

3   *"Die deutsche Polizei im Osteinsatz,"* Latvian State Historical Archives P-83-1-13, pp. 22–23.

Latvian *schutzmann.* Now he wanted to "settle scores" with his former competitors—Jews. More than once Heske Levinstein had defeated Holcmanis in the ring, and coaches had predicted a great future for him in boxing. Heske also was the only Jew who played for the local football team Olympia.

Now Holcmanis raised false charges against Heske with the SS. They arrested Heske and took him to town prison Nr. 2 (formerly the women's prison). Holcmanis met him in the prison yard and, together with other Nazis, pounced on him and started beating him severely. Heske realized this was the end. Gathering his last strength, he struck the boxer-policeman with a knock-out punch. When Holcmanis regained his consciousness, he shot Heske right on the spot, in the prison-yard.

The first mass shooting in the summer of 1941 was in Rainis Park, later ones were near the fishery port and the lighthouse or on the Naval base, and finally near the village of Šķēde, one kilometer north of the base on the Baltic coast. Then came the largest one, from 14 to 17 December, 1941, when 2,749 Jews were shot at Šķēde. It was ordered by the brutal police general Friedrich Jeckeln, newly appointed as Higher Police and SS-Chief for Ostland. He was to finish the job started by the *Einsatzgruppen,* and personally organized the killing of 24,000 Rīga Jews on 30 November and 8 December 1941 at Rumbula.

The Liepāja massacre, like most, had been planned and performed with German thoroughness, although the order had come only on 12 December. Latvian auxiliary police arrested the Jews and took them first to the women's prison and then to Šķēde, while German SD and Order Police oversaw matters in both places. In Šķēde, the Latvian auxiliary police contributed one firing squad; the other two were Latvian SD and a German platoon.

The executions were supervised by Carl-Emil Strott, the SD sergeant in charge (see photos on next page) who ran the operation with military precision. People were ordered to undress in the December cold (young women had to strip naked, older women only to their underwear), and Latvian policemen then led them to the ditch, where they stood facing the sea awaiting the firing squad's salvo. Most tumbled into the pit after being shot, but a Latvian policeman ("kicker") made the rounds from time to time and pushed bodies caught on the walls down into the pit.

Sobeck's pictures were saved for posterity by an audacious Jew, David Zivcon, who worked as an electrician in the SD building. Once he was told to repair the electric wiring in Sobeck's apartment. By chance he noticed a roll of film in a drawer and discovered that it contained twelve pictures of the December massacre. He smuggled them out, got a friend to make copies, and then returned the film by faking a power failure as a pretext for reentering the apartment. He hid the copies and turned them over to Soviet military intelligence after liberation. These pictures figured at the Nuremberg War Crimes Trial and have appeared in newspapers, books, and museum exhibits.

We—my mother, my younger brother, and I—were arrested at home on December 16 at about 2a.m. In those days, the widow and children of my paternal uncle Saul also stayed with us, as their house had been destroyed in the June battle for Liepāja. (Saul had been killed along with my father on 22.7.41).

The harsh sound of the door-bell, then blows at the door and shouts: "Open, or we'll break the door!" An SS-man burst into our apartment with six Latvian police: the German checks our names against the list, orders us to get dressed, take valuables with us, and leave the house. While we are getting ready, the policemen stuff everything that catches their eyes into their pockets.

When we were led out, it was dark in the street. We were taken to prison Nr. 2. When the convoy guard turned us over to the prison guard, he joked, "Here's another lot of Jews!" We went upstairs to the second floor. There sat a German SS-officer with two Latvian policemen. They told us to hand over our watches, money, rings, and any other valuables, and took the keys of our house as well. Our names were registered, and we were ordered to go back downstairs.

We found ourselves in the prison-yard, which was overcrowded with people. All of them were in hysterics: women were weeping and tearing their hair; children were crying; men were moaning, "This is the end!"

Among the crowd one could see Latvian policemen walking back and forth, beating people on their right and left with rubber truncheons. Jews were lined up in rows facing the wall. We had to stay there for hours without daring to turn around. If anybody crossed the yard to join his family for their last hour, the policemen immediately pounced on him and beat him with their truncheons.

Figure A3.1.   The Dec 15, 1941 executions at Škēde

Photographed by SS Oberscharführer Sobeck. [1] Five women posing, partly undressed before execution. (Several SS-men carried whips, and when they asked people to pose, they posed.) On the left, Sorella Epstein (10), hiding her face behind her mother Roza (43). Roza's husband Jakob had been shot in early July. [2] Another branch of the Epstein family, killed in a joint effort by Nazis and Soviets. Mia (18), like other young women, had to undress fully, and is sitting on the ground. Her mother Emma (47) and brother Max (15) are still undressing. Father Haim had been arrested by the NKVD in January 1941 and died in June 1942 in Saratov province. Note Latvian SD and police, with their armbands and rifles, everywhere. [3] Women running the gantlet. [4] The victims stood at the edge of the ditch facing the sea, while the firing squad took aim. [5,6] Most victims tumbled into the ditch, but those who didn't, were pushed in by a "kicker" (visible in pictures 5 and 6).

158

At dawn they started to drive us onto trucks, shouting and beating us with rifle-butts. The trucks kept coming to the prison at frequent intervals. All that lasted until 10–11 o'clock. People were taken to the Škēde dunes north of the navy base. They were lined up at ditches previously dug by Soviet POWs and shot.

Suddenly an SD-officer appeared in the prison-yard. He was accompanied by a navy officer named Kroll, who was supervisor at the *Korken-Fabrik* (cork factory), where some Jews worked.

The SD-officer shouted, "Those who work at the Korken-Fabrik, step to the right!" People hastened to draw up in formation.

My mother grabbed my brother, me, and my cousin by the hand and joined that group; we had nothing to lose at that moment.

Escorted by the navy officer, we were let out of the prison-yard. On the way we succeeded in separating from the group. Soon we returned home.

The December shootings caused consternation among the local population. They saw people brought to the prison and then to the execution site. They saw the returning trucks loaded with clothes of the executed people. And some policemen, when drunk, bragged how they had killed women, children, and babies.[4]

On 11 February 1942, they came for us again, at 9 o'clock in the evening. My aunt and her children having been killed in December, we now shared the apartment with another family, the Silbermans. They had been evicted from their apartment to make room for a German officer. It was a family of three: husband Israel, wife Golde, and daughter Sheine, my classmate.

A German police officer checked everybody's names and ordered us to get dressed. Latvian police were combing the apartment, shoving everything they wanted into their pockets.

My mother called me up to her and whispered, "Sjoma, run away! Perhaps you'll find some friends who will help you."

I got dressed and stole to the exit. But a Schutzmann was on guard there, another one guarded the other exit. So I slipped into one of the back rooms, quietly opened the window, and jumped down into the yard from the second floor.

February of 1942 was snowy and cold. SS-Untersturmführer Kügler, who had allegedly been on leave during the December *aktion*, himself took charge of the February shootings. He decided to send the victims to the execution site during the nightly curfew, to keep them out of people's view. Victims were arrested in the evening and taken to the women's prison. Under cover of darkness, they were sent to the execution site in horse-drawn sleighs.

Only once did the doomed people succeed in escaping, as reported by sergeant Lietzau of the German *Schutzpolizei*.[5] On 15 February 1942 at about midnight, a two-horse sleigh with sixteen "evacuated" (the Nazi euphemism for killed or about-to-be-killed) Jews was heading for a casemate on the naval base under the guard of two Latvian policemen, corporals Kalē[js] and Mag[n]us. When they approached the corner of Rīgas and Rainis streets, the Jews tackled the policemen and threw them off the sleigh. They also hit the driver over the head with the lantern, so that he, too, fell from the sleigh.

Only at 1:15a.m. did the bedraggled policemen report the incident to the officer-on-duty of the 21st police battalion. Several police patrols were promptly sent out to search for the fugitives, but with little success. Near the site of the incident they found a Jew who had been wounded in the head by a bullet and was unable to move. Finally, at 4:45a.m. a guard at the cadet school discovered the sleigh, with a two-year-old Jewish child in it. Both the wounded man and the child were taken to the women's prison, presumably to be "evacuated" at the next opportunity.

The fugitives fared better, at least for the time being. After driving along the main street, the Jews jumped off the sleigh and whipped the horses, sending them running in the opposite direction. Then the fugitives split into several groups and dispersed. As the incident happened in Jaun-Liepāja (the new part of town, north of the harbor canal), one group of the people went to nearby Tirgus Street 23, where Haim Kopman and the Hakel family lived. Kopman realized

---

4   In his biweekly progress report of 3 January 1942, Kügler had noted with disappointment: "The execution of Jews carried out during the report period still is the conversation topic of the local population. The fate of the Jews is widely deplored, and thus far few voices have been heard in favor of the elimination of the Jews." ("US Holocaust Memorial Museum" manuscript RG–18.002M, file 83-1-22).

5   Report of the 1st Police Precinct, 16. 2. 1942, Latvian State Historical Archives, P83-1-207, p. 112.

from the gentle knock at the door that these were not Nazis. He let them in and later led them to Hakel. When Hakel went to work early the next morning, he nonchalantly took them across the guarded bridge. Later the fugitives parted and stayed at different houses. Among them were Esja Horovitz, the teacher Abo Stolper with his wife Zara (née Matison) and son Shleima, as well as Jakob Merjam, who had hit the driver over the head with the lantern. Merjam is the only one who survived the war.

In the mid-February *aktion*, 152 Jews were killed at Šķēde (Ezergailis, p. 3 this volume). Among them were my mother Lyuba Feigerson (thirty-five), my younger brother Yossi Feigerson (five), and my cousin Reuven Traubin (six).

After my flight from our apartment I kept roaming about the town. But wherever I knocked, nobody let me in. After some hours of useless search I found myself near our house again. It was dark and still there. That night I made my way to Kuršu street where a Latvian family, the Evels, lived. My parents were on friendly terms with them. At the risk of their lives, the Evels hid me in their cellar. One week later, I went to town in search of any of my relatives. I found my mother's cousin Malka Munitz who lived in Tirgus laukums (Market square) with her two children. Her husband was killed together with my father in the Arājs *aktion* of 22–24 July 1941.

I stayed with the Munitz's for a while, working in a smithy in the naval base. Across the street from the Munitz's house there was an inn where farmers in town for the market used to leave their horses. In its courtyard stood a small house. One of my classmates and his sister lived in one of its rooms. After work I often crossed the street (during Jewish curfew hours) and stayed at my friend's for hours. One day we heard the sound of a car engine, looked out the window and saw the notorious van nicknamed "Black Bertha." The van stopped at the Munitzs's house, which I had just left. Some minutes later the police led Malka Munitz (thirty-eight) and her little children out.

It was clear that I could not stay there any longer. I ran into the apartment, picked up some necessities, and returned to my classmate. We were sure that a new shooting action had started. It was necessary to find another shelter. In the daytime we kept watching the street from the window, and at night we slept in the attic.

Nevertheless, the police (probably tipped off by a neighbor) seemed convinced that some Jews were hiding in the old inn. We watched them searching for us. They combed attic and cellar, piercing hay sheaves and even manure with their bayonets. We had to leave immediately and look for a new hiding place. We stayed either with Jews or with Latvians for a short while, but none of them dared give us shelter for long.

These arrests and murders continued until the opening of the ghetto. During one of the roundups, they arrested and sent to Šķēde Ida Fleishman, a running champion of the Makkabi sports club. She had already undressed and was being led to the pit when she suddenly started running in the direction of the navy base. SD-Scharführer August Kaiser chased after Ida. He had also been an athlete in the past. But he failed to overtake the girl. She slipped into a building where German sailors hid her.

But Kaiser had seen what door she had run into and demanded that the sailors surrender her. Otherwise he threatened to call the Gestapo. "The Jewish girl ran so fast, like a deer. But she must not be left alive: she has seen too much," he explained to the sailors. In the end, they surrendered Ida, and Kaiser took her back to the execution site.

The December 1941 and February 1942 executions had convinced the Jews of Liepāja that they were all doomed. From the early days of the occupation, families that did not want to undergo the humiliating execution procedure committed suicide by hanging, gas poisoning, or cutting their veins.

The April arrests and executions were timed to the Führer's birthday (20 April). The Liepāja SD caught Jews wherever they saw them and sent them straight to the execution site in Šķēde. That was how the teacher Abo Stolper and his wife (who had survived the memorable sleigh ride in February) were caught. This time there was no miracle; the Stolpers were killed.

In one of the trucks headed for Šķēde there was Shleime Havenson, a strong and brave young man. Shleime jumped off the moving truck and ran toward some bombed-out houses. He did not know that a passenger car with SD-men followed every such truck. They opened fire and wounded Shleime in the leg. He was delivered in fetters to the execution site.

As for me, my roaming continued until the very day the ghetto was opened, on 1 July 1942.

Figure A3.2.

Solomon Feigerson at the Soviet-era monument in Šķēde (August 1995). The inscription reads:

Here in 1941–45 the Hitlerite invaders killed in beastly manner more than 19,000 residents of Liepāja. IN ETERNAL MEMORY OF SOVIET PATRIOTS!

In the Soviet tradition, the number is grossly exaggerated, and there is no mention of Latvian participation in the killings, or the fact that most victims were killed as Jews, not as Soviet patriots

THE LIEPĀJA GHETTO

In the spring of 1942 the Liepāja newspaper "Kurzemes Vārds" reported: "The Jewish problem in Liepāja is completely solved. We got rid of the Jews. But if now and then we still find a Jew, we must show him the place he deserves." At the end of May 1942 the newspaper reminded the people: "It is necessary to dispose of the remaining Jews in our society!" It published an order requiring all Jews to move to a ghetto by 1 July.

By that time the majority of the Liepāja Jews had been shot. Among them were men who had fought for the independence of Latvia in the 1918–1920 war. People who had lived all their lives in that town—old men, women, and children—were killed just for being Jews by birth. When fewer than 1,000 Jews remained of the original 7,100, the authorities announced that a ghetto would be set up—something that had never before existed in Liepāja.

A "*Judenrat*" was formed, headed by Solomon Izraelit and his assistant, lawyer Monya Kaganski. Both were respected men who were eager to help every Jew. All Jews had to register with the *Judenrat* and move to the ghetto. The German and local authoritie's allotted one city block for the ghetto, bounded by Kungu, Bāriņu, Dārza and Apšu streets. In that block, there were thirteen houses, the inhabitants of which had previously moved into the apartments of executed Jews. Now Jews had to work on the construction of the ghetto in the evenings, after finishing their daily hard labor. They dug pits, put up posts, stretched barbed wire, and built a barbed-wire fence around the ghetto, properly symbolizing their status.

The SD knew that the Jews had to be accommodated for only a short time while their labor was needed; after Germany's final victory, there would be no place for them in the "New Europe." Meanwhile, the housing problem caused by the ravages of the June 1941 siege could be alleviated by cramming the Jews into tighter quarters.

The Judenrat assigned dwellings to the people. The quota of 4 m^2/person was less than half the skimpy quota of Soviet times, and so several families had to be jammed into each apartment. Partitions were built in some rooms to provide every family with its own corner. The Jews had to work hard cleaning and repairing everything, as the apartments vacated by Latvian families were in dismal condition.

When I heard that Jews had started constructing the ghetto, I came out of my "den" and joined them. We were just putting up a fence when the foreman of the crew, David Zivcon, called me. He led me into a deserted house and began to search me, as somebody had told him I had a handgun. In those days I never parted with my gun, planning to use the first bullet for any German or Latvian who tried to search me, and the second one, for myself. I was twelve years old and clearly understood what was in store for me. Zivcon took my gun away, beat me severely, and ordered me to resume my work. (Once after the war, when I chanced to meet David, I asked him, "Why did you beat me then?" He replied, "To scare you, so you would keep your mouth shut about the gun").

Right on schedule, on 1 July 1942, the remaining 832 Liepāja Jews found themselves behind the barbed wire of the ghetto. About 650 women and children were among them. Master Sergeant Kerscher from the *Schutzpolizei* was appointed commandant of the ghetto. When comparing his attitude with that of the Rīga commandant Krause, I think the Liepāja Jews were a bit luckier. The guards were Latvian auxiliary police. Everybody had to tell his number at the gate check-point when leaving the ghetto and returning. The guards kept watch over people, so that nobody could escape.

On coming to the ghetto, I (being alone) was accommodated in the hostel called "*Junggesellen-Heim*" (bachelors' hostel). That was a large room containing twenty beds. The inmates included some true bachelors (the war prevented some of them from settling down to married life) and some teenagers, but mainly people whose families had been killed while they were at work during an *aktion*. The Nazis decided to spare some of them for the time being, as they were useful craftsmen.

Life in the ghetto commenced. In the morning the columns went to work through the main gate, in the evening the returning people were counted and searched at the gate.

The Jews did their best to help each other. Many had known the others from pre-war times. People managed to preserve human dignity under these trying circumstances. Even women had to work hard in the rain and snow. In bitter frost they carried bricks and did other kinds of hard work.

After a while, I was assigned to the group that worked on the farm attached to the SD. I had to pasture cows, sweep the yard, work in the garden, etc. As I was near the Nazis every day, I memorized their names for life: the head of the Liepāja SD, SS-Untersturmführer W. Kügler and his assistant, Oberscharführer C. Strott.

Every day a column of Jews headed for the SD building (at Kūrmājas avenue 21) to do their assigned jobs: shoemakers made boots, and the jeweler Michael Libauer remade golden articles (confiscated from Jews before execution) for the SS officials. Being a very talented person, David Zivcon was a specialist for optics and electricity as well as an expert on cars, for which the Nazis valued him.

My job included the following: I took the cows at the SD building and drove them to beautiful places on the coastline. Before lunch I brought them back for milking, then took them back till the end of the working day. If the weather was bad, I sometimes came back earlier; and then had to clean the cow sheds, weed the grass in the garden, or wash cars. One of the motorcars was called "Black Bertha." It carried the arrested Jews. Everybody in the town knew it—a van of Soviet manufacture, "GAZ-AA"—that transported people to the shooting site. Occasionally, after Jews had resisted their murderers, its body was stained with blood and splattered brains.

The food supply in the ghetto was quite inadequate. The trifling pay in occupation Reichsmarks was spent on rationed food in a special shop inside the ghetto. So as not to die of hunger, Jews tried to barter their belongings for bread and other food when working outside the ghetto. When moving into the ghetto, they had been able to take some of their belongings that had not been confiscated, and local people grasped quickly that for a piece of bread they could get something valuable from the Jews. However, it was dangerous to carry those foodstuffs into the ghetto.

Once the Germans detained Mrs. Berta Rubinstein at the gates of the ghetto on her return from work, presumably because she was trying to bring in some food for her children. Her family had arrived in Liepāja in August 1939, together with other refugees from Germany. Her husband Oskar had been arrested during the major *aktion* in July 1941 (during which my father also fell in the hands of the Germans) and shot to death together with the other Jews. Mrs. Rubinstein, who by some miracle escaped the killings of 1941–42, came to the ghetto with her two little children. On the day after her arrest, SD-Scharführer Handke came to the ghetto and demanded that the head of the *Judenrat*, Mr. Israelit, give him Mrs. Rubinstein's children. Israelit led the boys to Handke's car. The children started to cry and begged uncle Israelit not to give them up, but let them wait till their mother returned. Handke got impatient, grabbed the boys, and threw them into the car. After a few days, we learned that the Nazis had shot Mrs. Rubinstein and her children.

In spite of all this, we somehow got accustomed to such a life. People managed to keep their folk wisdom, humor, and courage, but the hatred toward the enemy gradually built up. I don't remember exactly in what month, October or November, in 1942 a rumor spread that in the next few days all the apartments would be searched. People got panic-stricken. They started to hide their more valuable things and threw away the foodstuffs they had bartered outside the ghetto, the very items one could otherwise only dream of. Kalman Linkimer described those days in his famous song "The Waste Bin." The searching was terrible. The ghetto looked as if after a pogrom.

Nevertheless, life—if one could call it that—went on. The ghetto Jews did the dirtiest jobs and still cherished the hope for survival.

One day it became known that the ghetto food shop had been robbed. For those times that was an extraordinary event—Jews had robbed Jews. The Germans arrested and shot the robbers.

At the end of October 1942, some Jews from the Rīga ghetto were transported to the Liepāja ghetto, among them Jews from different countries—Lithuania, Poland, Czechoslovakia, Austria, and Germany. They were sent to work at the Liepāja sugar factory. The sugar-beet crop was quite large in 1942, but there was a shortage of workers in the factory, as most local Jews had already been killed.

The new arrivals told us of the massacres of Rīga and European Jews in late 1941, in which about 30,000 Jews were killed. The first mass murder occurred on 30 November 1941. People were driven on foot from the ghetto to the execution site in the Rumbula forest, about 10 km away. It was cold and dark, the road was covered with ice, and many people stumbled and fell. Others walking at their side caught them and dragged them along. Still, some people were left behind, and were shot by the Latvian police escorts, who kept driving the others while shouting: "Faster, faster, or we'll shoot." The place on the edge of the forest, to which long columns of the Jews—men, women, and children—were driven was cordoned off by German soldiers and Latvian police. At daybreak, they started the killing.

For such massacres, Jews from the occupied countries of Europe and from Germany proper had been brought to Latvia. Both the Germans and their local collaborators became notorious as specialists in killing people. Besides shootings, gas vans were used for this purpose. The sites of mass murder were: the railway station Šķirotava and the Biķernieku and Rumbula forests in the outskirts of Rīga.

The Liepāja Jews greeted the newcomers like relatives, sharing their last food and clothes with them, inviting them to their homes. Every meeting of that kind started with stories relating to their native homes where they had lived before the Nazis came to power.

The work at the sugar factory was very hard, in three shifts. The Jews from the Rīga ghetto worked in Liepāja until February 1943, when they were transported back to Rīga. The parting was not easy; people knew what awaited them. The tailor Gurevich even wrote a song in Yiddish to the music of "Centralka" (The Rīga Central prison):

> "Rīga townsfolk, you favored us with gleams of happiness,
> We won't ever forget how we were together, during all those hard days."

Life in the ghetto continued. People went out to work at dawn and returned late at night. One needed additional strength for housekeeping. We illegally listened to the radio in the ghetto, spreading the news by word of mouth, and thus knew about the German defeat at Stalingrad in January–February 1943. But we had no inkling of the uprising in the Warsaw ghetto in April 1943.

There were lots of courageous people in the Liepāja ghetto. Being completely isolated from the rest of the world, the Jews lived like one family, rendering support to one another, sometimes even at the risk of their lives.

After the revolt in the Warsaw ghetto, Himmler decreed that all the ghettos in the occupied territories should be liquidated. In the second half of September 1943, ghetto commandant Kerscher announced that the remaining Jews would be transported to Rīga. There were rumors in the ghetto that this was a prelude to complete extermination; people got worried. On 3 October 1943 two couples—David and Henni Zivcon, Michael and Hilda Skutelsky—managed to escape from the ghetto to a courageous man, Roberts Sedols, who had prepared his cellar as a long-term shelter for Jews. Some time later the four escapees were joined by Aaron Vesterman, Zelik Hirschberg, Kalman Linkimer, Misha Libauer, Yosif Mendelstam, and Shmerl Skutelsky. Altogether Roberts Sedols provided shelter to eleven people, but he himself did not live to see the end of the war: he was killed by shrapnel in March 1945.

Figure A3.3. The plaque inside the former Liepāja ghetto:
Between Kungu, Apšu, Dārza, and Bāriņu streets
from 1 July 1942 to 8 October, 1943
was the ghetto for the doomed Liepāja Jews.

On 8 October 1943 the inhabitants of the Liepāja ghetto were ordered to gather at the gate with their belongings early in the morning. The Jews, from children to old men, were drawn up in a column and driven to the local train station, under escort of SD-men and Latvian police. Freight cars were waiting for them. After driving the last Jew onto the train, SD Scharführer Handke put up a sign on the station wall: *"Libau Judenfrei!"* (Liepāja free of Jews!)

For this final expulsion the Nazis chose the most sacred day of the Jewish people: Yom Kippur

THE TERRIBLE BUT UNFORGOTTEN PAST

On 8 May 2000, the anti-Hitler coalition celebrated the fifty-fifth anniversary of victory over Hitler Germany. Everybody who experienced and survived that terrible time will remember that day forever. The war finally ended. Fifty-five years have passed since the end of that horror.

They say, time heals old wounds. Still, there are wounds that keep bleeding and do not let one forget the evil that had been inflicted.

Is it ever possible to forget the crimes committed by Hitler and his gang?

Is it ever possible to calm down and say, "Yes, that was an evil dream, a nightmare that will never be repeated"?

That is why we, those who were condemned to pass through all the circles of the Nazi hell, which had many names, must keep that memory and remind all mankind of the tragedy of our nation.

First place in the devil's list belongs to Auschwitz, the second one to Treblinka, with its bloody ballast. Then come Bergen-Belsen, Chelmno, Sachsenhausen, Ravensbrück, Neuengamme, Flossenburg, Stutthof, Dora, Mauthausen, and all the others.

The ground of the camps is covered with the ashes of millions of people who had been killed by exhaustion at forced labor or on the roll-call grounds, suffocated in gas chambers, or shot to death, and burned in crematorium ovens. For those prisoners who had not survived, victory over Nazi Germany came too late.

Most concentration camps had already been liberated before the end of the war. In January 1945 the Soviet army liberated Auschwitz. The camps in Germany and Austria were liberated by the Allies in April–May 1945. But at that very time hundreds of thousands of prisoners were being driven along the roads deep into Germany and Austria, without any water or food. Tens of thousands of Jews perished on the way. The weak ones were shot; many others died of cold, hunger, and disease. The sight of the liberated concentration camps made a searing impression on Allied soldiers and officers. There were mountains of bodies the Nazis had had no time to burn. Terribly distorted corpses were scattered all over the camp. Living skeletons gazed at the liberators. In those camps people were killed because they were human beings, because they were innocent.

Life in those camps was much more difficult for us Jews than for other prisoners, as we were tortured both as an inferior race destined for destruction and as criminals. Our sole crime consisted of being born by Jewish mothers.

The liberation of mass murder camps by the Allied troops was of great human and historical importance, though it is still being argued about today. Even after the passage of fifty-five years since that terrible time, nobody and nothing is forgotten.

The Author

Solomon (Sjoma) Feigerson was born 16 November 1930 in Liepāja, Latvia. After liberation on 3 May 1945, he returned to Latvia, settling in Rīga where he resumed his education at an evening school. He married Ethel in 1957. Their son Yakov was born in 1960. In 1963 he entered the Faculty of Mechanics, graduating in 1969 as a mechanical engineer. For fifteen years he had been working at the Rīga plant "Impuls."

In 1966 Feigerson and his family began to prepare for Aliyah to Israel. After many refusals of an exit permit, they finally arrived in Israel on June 1, 1971. For the next twenty-six years he worked as an engineer at the plant "Telrad." He retired in Rishon Le Zion, Israel, where he died on Feb. 24, 2010.

Δ Δ Δ

Comment

BY EDWARD ANDERS

Some of the murderers got their deserved punishment. Walter Stahlecker, who commanded Einsatzgruppe A that killed 35,000 Jews in Latvia, was fatally wounded by a partisan's bullet near Leningrad in 1942. Friedrich Jeckeln, who killed more than 30,000 in Rumbula, Šķēde, and elsewhere, was hanged in Rīga in 1946. Wolfgang Kügler, head of the Liepāja SD, committed suicide in a West German jail on 2.12.1959. Several other members of the Liepāja SD were tried in Hannover in 1969/71, but got off lightly. Strott—by then a retired hotel director—got only a seven-year prison term, and Grauel, Reiche, Kuketta, Fahrbach, and Rosenstock, one and a half to six years. Baumgartner, who was tried in East Berlin, was sentenced to death.

I do not know which of the murderers of Kaiserwald and Stutthof were brought to justice, and what the outcome was. The arch-murderer Viktors Arājs was inexplicably released from British detention in 1948 and lived peacefully in Frankfurt under his wife's maiden name for twenty-seven years. He was apprehended in 1975 and sentenced to life imprisonment (after 199 sessions of the court[6]), but died in 1986. I worked in the War Crimes section of the Federation of Liberated Latvian Jews in Munich in 1948, and helped my counterpart in London, H. Michelson, gather evidence against Arājs and other war criminals. Regrettably, this effort was sabotaged by a Jewish organization that voted to end the London operation, fearing—without any reason whatsoever—that the British government might ban food parcels to survivors if they didn't stop the hunt for war criminals.

---

6   Andrew Ezergailis, "The Holocaust in Latvia 1941–1944." Rīga: The Historical Institute of Latvia, 1996.

The Soviets tried about three hundred members of the Arājs Commando, most of whom got ten to twenty-five years in the Gulag or the death penalty.[7] They also tried a number of *schutzmänner*, but given the arbitrariness of Soviet justice, and the attitude that killing Jews is a less serious crime than killing others, some sentences may have been too lenient and others too harsh.

Many murderers got to the West, and most of them escaped punishment. A significant number went insane,[8] which is not a bad substitute for the gallows. Efforts should continue to track down and prosecute murderers. But prospects of conviction get smaller every year, as it becomes harder to prove—to the high standards of Western courts—that a given SS man or Schutzmann pulled the trigger sixty years ago. Whether we like it or not, most of the remaining ones will die peacefully in their beds. While not giving up the hunt for murderers, we should look to the future and try to ensure that the murderers' spirit does not live on among the young people of Latvia and other countries. Holocaust education is being introduced into Latvian schools, and we must hope that just as in Germany, the young generation will condemn the sins of the evildoers of the wartime generation, and fight the racists and hatemongers of their own generation. We can help this process by making a clear distinction between guilty and innocent Latvians and Germans.

Biographical Summary: Edward Anders (Added by kwk)

Edward Anders (originally Eduard Alperovitch) was born in Liepāja, Latvia, in 1926, as the second son of the grain exporter Adolf Alperovitch and Erika Löwenthal. On 14 June 1941, the family narrowly escaped deportation to the USSR. After the German invasion on 22 June 1941, Erika falsely claimed that she was an aryan foundling, which made her sons half-Jews and enabled them to avoid most of the anti-Jewish persecutions. His father and all twenty-four other relatives who were still in Latvia perished during the Holocaust. Erika and Edward left Latvia before the advancing Red Army in October 1944, pretended to be ethnic Germans on arrival to Germany, and thus survived the war. Edward and his mother immigrated to the US in 1949, where Edward received a PhD in Chemistry from Columbia University, New York, in 1954.

From 1955 to 1991 he was on the faculty of the University of Chicago, where he became Professor of Chemistry in 1962. With his students, he did research on the composition, age, and origin of meteorites and lunar rocks, resulting in about 270 publications. Among their discoveries is a huge fire that was triggered by the impact of a giant meteorite 65 million years ago and contributed to the mass extinction of more than two-thirds of all living species. They also isolated traces of "stardust" from primitive meteorites: tiny grains of diamond, graphite, and other minerals that formed outside the solar system. This work has provided much new information on nuclear processes in stars.

Anders has received various professional honors, including membership in the US National Academy of Sciences. On his retirement in 1991, he and his wife Joan moved to Bern, Switzerland, but returned to the US in 1999 and now live in Burlingame, California. They have two children: George Anders (b. 1957) and Nanci Schiman (b. 1959). After his retirement he urged a survivors' organization to recover the names of Liepāja Holocaust victims from archives in Riga, but when the organization showed no interest, he organized and financed the project himself. Since 1996 he has worked on various remembrance projects for Holocaust and Gulag victims from his home town.

---

7   R. Vīksne, "NKVD/KGB Trials of Arājs Commando Members." In: *The Issues of the Research of the Holocaust in Latvia (Materials of an International Conference, 16–17.10.2000, Rīga, Latvia).* Riga: Latvian History Institute Press, 2000.

BIBLIOGRAPHY AND FURTHER READING

CHAPTER 3. LITHUANIAN JEWS AND GRAUDAN FAMILY IN PANEVEZYS

Books

Aaron, Sam. *Jewish Ancestors: A Guide to Jewish Genealogy in Lithuania.* London: Jewish Genealogical Society of Great Britain, 2005.

Greenbaum, Masha. *The Jews of Lithuania. A History of a Remarkable Community 1316–1945.* , Jerusalem, NY: Gefen Publishing House, 1995.

Levin, Dov. *The Litvaks. A Short History of the Jews in Lithuania.* Jerusalem: Yad Vashem Publications, 2001.

Articles

Gaidis, Henry L. "Napoleon's Lithuanian Forces," *Lituanus, Lithuanian Quarterly Journal of Arts and Sciences*, 1984; 30(1); http://www.lituanus.org/1984_1/84_1_01.htm

Ofek, Adina: "Cantonists: Jewish Children as Soldiers in Tsar Nicholas's Army," *Modern Judaism.* Oxford: Oxford University Press, 1993; vol. 13 (no. 3): 277–308; http://www.jstor.org/stable/1396327

Web

"Jewish Communities and Box and Candle Tax Lists." www.jewishgen.org/litvak/html/vital-p4.htm

Kaplan, Rochelle. "Korobka Tax on Kraziai' Jews," Document 49-1-1362 from the Kauna Archive. http://www.shtetlinks.jewishgen.org/Kraziai/history_tax_on_jews.htm

Leeson, Dan. "Military Conscription in Russia in the 19th Century." A JewishGen InfoFile 1995; http://www.jewishgen.org/infofiles/ru-mil.txt

Palomino, Michael. "Cantonist Children for the Russian Army (17th century until 1856)—Prosecution of the Jews." Presentation 2007, *Encyclopaedia Judaica*, 1971:5; http://www.geschichteinchronologie.ch/russland-bis-1917/EncJud_ansiedlungsrayon03a-kantonistenkinder-17jh-1856-ENGL.html

Rosenthal, Herman and J.G. Lipman. "Korobka." JewishEncyclopedia.com, 2002; http://www.jewishencyclopedia.com/view.jsp?artid=373&letter=K

Schuyler, Eugene. "Eugene Schuyler's 1872 letter on the Legal Position of the Hebrews in Russia." Source: House of Representatives Executive Document No. 192, 47th Congress, 1st Session, Serial Set 2030; http://www.angelfire.com/ms2/belaroots/schuyler.htm

CHAPTERS 5 AND 7: LATVIAN JEWS AND THE GRAUDAN FAMILY IN LIBAU

Books

Anders, Edward and Juris Dubrovskis. *Jews in Liepāja, Latvia 1941–45: A Memorial Book*. Burlingame, CA: Anders Press, 2001.

Beare, Arlene. *A Guide to Jewish Genealogy in Latvia and Estonia*. London: Jewish Genealogical Society of Great Britain, 2001.

Ezergailis, Andrew. *The Holocaust in Latvia 1941–1944: The Missing Center*. Washington DC: United States Holocaust Memorial Museum, 1996.

Press, Berndard. *The Murder of the Jews in Latvia 1941–1945*. Evanston, Illinois: Northwestern University Press, 2000.

Web

Anders, Edward. "Jews in Liepāja/Latvia, 1941–45: A Database of Victims and Survivors;" www.liepajajews.org

Herzenberg, Leonardo. "Robert Herzenberg Memoirs." Chicago: Leo and Carol Herzenberg. www.herzenberg.net

APPENDIX 1

Herzenberg, Leonardo. "Robert Herzenberg Memoirs." Chicago: Leo and Carol Herzenberg. www.herzenberg.net

APPENDIX 3

Feigerson, Solomon. *The Tragic Fate of Liepāja Jews*. From Edward Anders and Juris Dubrovskis, *Jews in Liepāja, Latvia 1941–45: A Memorial Book*. Burlingame, CA: Anders Press, 2001.